Downfall and Deliverance

by LEON J. WOOD

This book has been prepared primarily for group study in connection with the Adult Teacher's Guide available for 60¢ from Regular Baptist Press. However, it is also an excellent and informative book to use for individual instruction.

Published
by
REGULAR BAPTIST PRESS
1800 Oakton Boulevard
Des Plaines, Illinois 60018

CONTENTS

Foreword . . . . Inside front cover

Chapters

1. Introduction to the Book 1
2. The Sin of Israel 11
3. The First Two Oppressions 22
4. Deborah and Barak Against Sisera . . 32
5. The Man Gideon 42
6. The Defeat of the Midianites 52
7. Aftermath of Victory 62
8. Abimelech, the Renegade King 71
9. Jephthah and the Ammonites 80
10. Samson the Strong 89
11. Samson's Success and Failure 99
12. Micah and the Danites 108
13. Civil War in Israel 118

Copyright 1975 by Regular Baptist Press. Vol. 23, No. 3. Printed in U.S.A. Dr. Merle R. Hull, Executive Editor; Ruth Herriman, Managing Editor.

CHAPTER 1

Introduction to the Book

BIBLE PORTIONS TO READ: Joshua 24:1-33; the Book of Judges

WE ARE ABOUT TO LEARN something about the Book of Judges and the period of history it records.

I. Character of the Period

The Book of Judges records what transpired between Joshua's death and Samuel's ministry. This era is often referred to as the Period of the Judges because twelve people—called judges—served as leaders during this time.

A. A Theocratic Form of Government

The Period of the Judges lasted about four centuries. It was unique in that it was a period of great promise, but it resulted in tragic disappointment.

During this time God led His people in a manner different from other nations. The nations around them had earthly kings; but God wanted Israel to look to Him as their sole Ruler. Thus He prescribed for them a minimum of earthly government. Cities had their elders for general supervisory work, and the land as a whole had the religious leadership of priests and Levites. But there was no central king, no central government; and even the separate tribes had no governors over them. Most cities had a local court composed of "judges and officers" (Deut. 16:18) to decide cases. They apparently shared these with the elders. There was also a sort of supreme court (Deut. 17:8ff.) composed of priests and lay judges, serving at the central Tabernacle. These presumably decided the more difficult cases.

This form of government—with God as sole Ruler—is called a theocracy. God desired this for His people. It would cause them to depend completely on Him.

Today, too, God wants His children to look to Him to supply all life's needs.

B. The Priests and Levites

Under a theocratic form of government the priests and Levites were God's special representatives on earth. They were given forty-eight cities—evenly distributed among the tribes (Num. 35:1-8; Josh. 21:1-41)—in which to dwell. They were near the people to instruct and counsel them. At set times during the year the priests and Levites served at the central Tabernacle, residing there for the assigned period. The Tabernacle was located at Shiloh. This was central geographically; so all the people had equal access to it.

God established the Tabernacle in such a central place to unify the tribes. The tribes were separate entities, but God wanted them to sense their historic and essential oneness. They should find this in God Who had chosen them in Abraham, and the Tabernacle should serve as the earthly instrument through which this oneness could be expressed. Persons from all the tribes were to bring their individual sacrifices there, and all male citizens were to appear there personally every year at three main feasts—Passover, Pentecost and Tabernacles (Exod. 23:14-17).

C. No Need of Taxes

Had the people followed God's will in these matters, they would have prospered spiritually and materially.

Through all the ages of time, people have been burdened with high government taxes. But if Israel had followed God's plan during this Period of the Judges, the people would not have had to pay taxes. There was no government to support. Even the elders likely earned their own living. Therefore, when the people asked Samuel for a king, God gave them one but told Samuel to warn them that they would have to pay taxes. The king would demand the best of their fields, vineyards and oliveyards and would take a tenth of their seed, their produce, etc. (1 Sam. 8:11-18).

If God's children of any day would learn that God's way is *always* best, they would enjoy better lives. It is easy for the Christian to reason in this way: If I put more time into my material affairs, I will profit more. However, if this entails doing less for God, it is a sad mistake. God's blessing comes only when one gives God's will and pleasure highest priority.

II. Historical Background

The twelve tribes of Israel were the descendants of Jacob's family. During a time of severe famine—and with God's approval (Gen. 46:2-4)—Jacob and his family journeyed to reside in Egypt where his son Joseph was the prime minister. The family stayed there 430 years (Exod. 12:40), their number growing to more than two million. Most of this time they were in grievous bondage to Egypt; but finally—under Moses' leadership—the people moved out from the land. By means of a cloud, God led them first to Mount Sinai where He gave them His Law. There, too, they built the Tabernacle which they carried with them to the Promised Land.

After the year at Mount Sinai the people were led to Kadesh-barnea from which they were directed to move on and conquer Canaan, but they refused to obey. They became fearful of the strong people, the walled cities and the giant Anakim which their reconnaissance party of twelve found (Num. 13:28). God punished them for disobeying by making them wander in the desert wilderness for forty years. During this time all persons twenty years old and over at the time of the disobedience died. Only a younger generation entered the land at last. Joshua led the remaining Israelites in. He and Caleb of the original reconnaissance group were the ones who had urged the people to do as God commanded. These two were the only ones God permitted to continue to live. The conquest of the land was completed in several months. There were victories at Jericho, Ai, the southern cities of the land as a group and over the northern cities in a similar manner. After the conquest, the land was allotted among the tribes. Joshua died shortly thereafter, and the story of the Judges began.

The immediate task which lay before the tribes was the actual occupation of the allotted territories. Joshua's victories had broken the strength of the native inhabitants, but they had not yet been displaced. Each tribe had to occupy its own territory.

III. The Religious Condition

A. At the Beginning of the Period

Note the religious condition of the people at the beginning of the Period of the Judges. The stress of this book is on the people's sinfulness. They became cold toward God, and many of them even worshiped Baal, the false god of the Canaanites. What was the condition, however, at the beginning of the period?

1. *Early Victories*

When one compares Israel at the beginning of the Period of the Judges with the deterioration toward the end, it began quite well. This is especially evident because of the degree of God's blessing. Scripture makes it clear that God doesn't bless His people who are far from Him. But God did bless in the wars of conquest, both those of Moses and of Joshua.

Under Moses two powerful kings—Sihon, king of the Amorites (Num. 21:21-31), and Og, king of Bashan

(Num. 21:32-35)—were defeated. Victories over them in two successive battles gave Israel possession of land east of the Jordan, from the Arnon River in the south to Mount Hermon in the north. Both kings were strong, but Moses' forces defeated them.

Then under Joshua there was the great victory over Jericho when God caused the walls of the fortress to fall. This was followed by the capture of Ai which came on the second attempt due to the hindering sin of Achan the first time (Josh. 7:1—8:29). After this there was the sweeping conquest of all the southern part of the land. At this time God caused a miraculous prolongation of daylight so the enemy would be defeated (Josh. 10:7-27). Finally there was the great victory over the northern region where Jabin, king of Hazor, was the main leader (Josh. 11:1-15).

2. *Resultant Reputation*

Israel's strength, as demonstrated in these conquests, gave the nation a high reputation among the native inhabitants. The Canaanites were made to fear. When the Israelite spies came to Jericho, they found the citizens there trembling for fear of the invaders (Josh. 2:8-11).

Then the people of Gibeon, a strong city of central Canaan, asked Joshua for a treaty of peace with the Israelites because the inhabitants were so fearful (Josh. 9:3-16). The Gibeonites used deceit to bring this about, and Joshua and the elders were at fault in being fooled. The Gibeonites sued for peace in this way because they feared Israel so greatly. Actually their capitulation gave Israel control of an important bastion in the middle of the country.

Later still the miracle of the prolonged day added further to the high reputation these people held for Israel and God. All this points up the fact that as Israel completed the conquest, she stood high in the estimation of the native inhabitants. This was the result of God's signal blessing, indicating that the people's spiritual condition was comparatively good.

B. The Change That Ensued

This changed, however, shortly after the death of Joshua and his generation. Compare Judges 2:7 with Judges 2:10 and 11. The people turned from God, and many began to serve Baal, the false god of the Canaanites. When they did this, God immediately withdrew His blessing. Then the troubles set forth in the Book of Judges were permitted to come.

C. An Important Lesson

Notice one of the most important lessons of the book here. It is that God blesses when His people remain in the place of blessing, but He does not when they leave that place. When Christians today live for the Lord and do His will, God is near to protect and provide. When they do not do this but let sin crowd into their lives, God's gracious presence is withdrawn. They do not lose their salvation, for God's family tie cannot be broken. However, they lose the reality of fellowship and joy as God's children. Often God permits chastisement of severe degree to come into their lives so they may be brought back to God (Heb. 12:3-15). God is not pleased with the chastisement which He must permit at such times. He would rather bring blessing than permit chastisement. But the need to check the sinning Christian in his way requires that unpleasant measures be taken.

IV. The Worship of Baal

Because Baal worship was a large factor in Israel's defecting from God during the period before us, we must note it particularly. What was there about Baal worship that attracted the Israelites? Why did they forsake the worship of the true God in order to worship this false one?

A. Baal, the God of Rainfall

The Canaanites believed Baal to be the god of storm and rainfall. Every Canaanite farmer had to worship and please Baal if he was to be assured of having rain to water his crops. The Israelites listened to this line of thinking as they became acquainted with the former inhabitants. God had strongly warned the Israelites against permitting these people to continue to live in the land (Num. 33:51-56) so they would not be tempted to follow the enemies' ways (Deut. 12:29-32). God knew that if they did not drive out the Baal worshipers, Israel would give ear to them.

B. The Attraction of Baal Worship

Because the Israelites didn't obey God but let the Canaanites continue to live in the land, they believed they could learn the best ways of farming from them. In Egypt their fathers had farmed through irrigation because the land was flat (Deut. 11:10); but this was not possible in Canaan which was hilly, calling for watering by "the rain of heaven" (Deut. 11:11). To farm hills, one must terrace the land. The Israelites apparently thought it was natural to learn how to terrace from the former inhabitants. But when they inquired of them, the Canaanites not only gave them technical advice but also told them they must worship Baal if they were to be assured of the necessary rainfall. Since rainfall was essential to good crops and since good crops were such a factor in material prosperity, many Israelites were persuaded to do as they were told. They followed the false way of worship, forsaking the true God in Heaven Who alone could give them the rain they needed.

C. The Sinfulness of Baal Worship

To worship Baal was to deny the true God. By going after Baal the people were breaking the First Commandment (Exod. 20:3). In itself this would have been serious. But there was more. Baal worship was a highly licentious form of worship. Fertility rites, involving religious prostitution, played a major role. The people thought these rites would enhance fertility in animal reproduction and bounteous crops. Without question many Israelites became involved in these rites as they sought to follow the pagan ways so they could prosper. Consequently the total religious program was a terrible offense to God. No wonder His blessing had to be withheld and chastisement had to be meted out.

V. The Purpose of the Book of Judges

A. A Record of Israelite Defection

Sometimes the Book of Judges is called the history book of the Judges' period, for what history is given in the Bible of this period is largely found in this book. The purpose of the book, however, is not to give this history but rather to give the story of Israel's defection and sin before God as existent during the period. The history set forth was selected to tell that story. A brief survey of the contents of the book will reveal this fact.

B. A Survey of the Contents

In chapter 1 the tribes' failure to fully occupy their allotted territories is the subject. As already noted, God's will was that each one would do this by driving out the former inhabitants. They sinned in not doing so. In chapter 2 a general introductory statement is made concerning Israel's sin for the overall period. It is said that the people did turn from God after the death of Joshua's generation. They then followed Baal, for which reason "they were greatly distressed" (v. 15). Therefore, judges were raised up to bring deliverance (vv. 16-19).

Chapter 3 brings the occasions of distress as enemy forces were allowed to bring defeat and oppression. The first oppression came from the Mesopotamians (3:7, 8). Othniel, the nephew of Caleb, was the judge raised up to bring deliverance (3:9-11).

The second oppression came from the Moabites across the Jordan to the east (3:12-14). Ehud of Benjamin killed Eglon, king of the enemy force, to deliver Israel from this oppressor (3:15-30).

The third oppression came from the Canaanites within the land proper. It was led by Sisera and his nine hundred chariots of iron (4:1-3). Deborah and Barak moved against him in a battle near Megiddo, bringing the desired victory (4:4-24).

The fourth period of distress came from the Midianites—again from east of the Jordan (6:1-6). This time Gideon was the chosen deliverer, and he brought relief through the remarkable victory of three hundred select men (6:11—8:21).

The fifth oppression came from the Ammonites, the third transjordan foe (10:7-18). Jephthah was the one used by God this time, and he won a signal victory after making a vow involving his only daughter which led to great distress (11:1-40).

The sixth and last period of distress came at the hands of the Philistines (10:7; 13:1) who lived in the southwest of Canaan near the Mediterranean. This time Samson was Israel's champion. Through prodigious feats of strength, he effected distress and confusion for the Philistines, thus hindering them from conquering Israel as they desired (13:2—16:31).

The last five chapters of the book relate two stories which illustrate the degree of sinfulness during the period. Though they conclude the book, both actually occurred early during the period. The one story concerns the tribe of Dan's disobediently moving from their allotted portion in the southwest to a region far north of the Sea of Galilee (Judg. 17:1—18:31). That the story occurred early is indicated by its being mentioned in the Book of Joshua (Josh. 19:47), and that book was written while Rahab of Jericho yet lived (Josh. 6:25).

The second story concerns the violation of a concubine of a certain Levite by men of Gibeah and the resultant war with Benjamin by the other tribes (Judg. 19:1—21:25). Also it must be placed early because Phinehas, who was active even before the time of conquest (Num. 25:7; Josh. 22:13, 31f), was still high priest (Judg. 20:28).

The two stories just mentioned are likely representative of many others that show concrete examples of the people's sinfulness.

C. The Rationale

The entire Book of Judges, then, involves sin and its consequences. God was saying that the reason His people, whom He wished to bless, were not blessed was because of their great sin. His chosen people, who had held such great promise of being prosperous and admired, did not experience this wonderful status because they forfeited it for the price of sin. The book is devoted to showing the reason Israel experienced the opposite of blessing. It stands as one of the great books of the Bible in warning against the awful cost of sinning against God.

Prepare To Answer Intelligently

1. Approximately how long did the Period of the Judges last?
2. Why didn't God give the people a king during the Period of the Judges?
3. Where was the Tabernacle located during the Judges' period?
4. Where did the priests and Levites live?
5. Why did the Israelites not have to pay taxes during this period?
6. What was the first task of the tribes after Joshua's death?
7. Characterize the reputation the Israelites had among the Canaanites at the time of Joshua's death.
8. Why were the Israelites so attracted to Baal worship?
9. What was the purpose in writing the Book of Judges?
10. What was the particular purpose of including the stories in the last five chapters?

CHAPTER 2

The Sin of Israel

BIBLE PORTION TO READ: Judges 1:1—2:23

AS IMPLIED in the first lesson we studied, the Book of Judges is divided into three sections. The first, covering chapters 1 and 2, is general in its reference to the sin of the period and introduces the book. The second, covering chapters 3 through 16, sets forth the overall history of the period, dealing especially with the times of oppression and deliverance. The third, covering chapters 17 through 21, tells two representative stories which illustrate the type of sin committed.

The first section is studied in this lesson. It is divided into two parts: the incomplete occupation of the land and a general statement regarding the people's sinfulness during the period.

I. Incomplete Occupation of the Land (Judg. 1:1—2:5)

Joshua had done well in breaking the strength of the land's fighting forces. The individual tribes, however, after being allotted their respective portions, did not move in to settle all that was assigned to them. This story is told in three steps: first, the failure of Judah and Simeon in particular; second, the failure of the other tribes and, third, the rebuke of the people and their remorse for the sin.

A. The Failure of Judah and Simeon in Particular (1:1-20)

The story of Judah's and Simeon's failure in occupying the portion of their allotment is told in greater detail than that of the others. The reason may be to give a concrete illustration of the failures which were true of all. The reason Judah and Simeon were the ones selected may be twofold: They were the first assigned to take up the task (1:2, 3), and they probably succeeded as well as any in the effort. Emphasizing their account, then, presented the overall picture in as favorable a light as possible. God was gracious in reporting the events, for the account of Judah and Simeon stressed their success rather than their failure.

1. *A Good Beginning (1:1-3)*

Joshua was dead. The people of Israel made a good beginning by recognizing the task before them and inquiring as to who should be the first to begin occupying. God replied, probably through the Urim and Thummim (Exod. 28:30; Num. 27:21), that Judah should go first. Judah was the largest tribe (Num. 26:22) and had been allotted its territory first (Josh. 15:1-63). Judah asked Simeon to assist in the task. This was done because the tribe of Simeon had been allotted cities in Judah as their portion (Josh. 19:1-9). The two tribes fought side by side in commendable fashion to occupy their territories.

2. *Defeat of Adonibezek (1:4-7)*

The first engagement was with the people of Bezek, made up of Canaanites and Perizzites, under the leadership of Adonibezek (meaning "Lord of Bezek"). Bezek may be identified with the present ruin *Bezkah,* located near Gezer. Some 10,000 of the enemy were killed, and the king was caught as he fled. His thumbs and great toes were cut off (v. 6) in the manner which he himself had followed with his enemies (v. 7). Adonibezek claimed to have conquered seventy kings prior to this time, indicating that he himself was a strong ruler. Thus the fact that Judah and Simeon were able to defeat him shows that their combined forces were formidable. But even more it indicates that God's blessing was still on the people at this time (v. 4). So long as the Israelites won in their battles, we know God was with them, bringing this about. However, as soon as they began to lose, we know that His favor had been withdrawn.

3. *Capture of Jerusalem (1:8)*

Verse 8, as translated in the King James Version, indicates that Jerusalem had been captured prior to this time. However, Joshua had not accomplished this in his earlier southern campaign, and there is no reason to believe that it had been done since. The verse is better translated: "Then the children of Judah fought against Jerusalem and captured it and smote it with the edge of the sword and set the city on fire." So then this taking of Jerusalem was simply the next step in the campaign of conquest.

Adonibezek was brought along to the city as the two tribes made their approach for the attack (v. 7). Jerusalem was captured at this time, but it was not held for long. Verse 21 states that "the children of Benjamin did not drive out the Jebusites that inhabited Jerusalem." Probably the Jebusites were able to win it back from the Israelites shortly after its capture here. Then it remained in Jebusite hands until David captured it and occupied it continuously as the capital of his new kingdom (2 Sam. 5:6-9).

4. *Capture of the Land Proper (1:9-20)*

Jerusalem, which had been allotted to Benjamin (1:21), and probably Bezek were not located in the land assigned to Judah and Simeon. Therefore, these battles were preparatory for the occupation itself. Perhaps both places were especially strong, and it was believed they should be defeated before God's people would be safe to move farther south. But now the combined army did move south into the allotted land itself. Hebron and Debir were captured first. The latter was captured through a special assignment to Othniel, nephew of Caleb. By capturing it, he won the hand of Caleb's daughter, Achsah. She asked her father for a field containing valuable springs of water, and he gave it to her. Compare this record with that in Joshua 15:13-19 and 14:6-15. It seems that this campaign at Hebron and Debir was primarily under the direction of Caleb, a member of the tribe of Judah, and that he used primarily his own family.

According to 1:16, descendants of Moses' father-in-law, Jethro, who evidently had accompanied the Israelites through the wilderness as far as Jericho, "the city of palm trees" (cf. Deut. 34:3), now moved into the south of the land. Then, according to verses 17 and 18, the Judah-Simeon forces captured the cities of Zephath (now called Hormah), Gaza, Askelon and Ekron. Verse 20 simply adds that Caleb received Hebron as already indicated in Joshua 14:6-15.

5. *The Failure (1:19)*

After this stress on success, the account speaks briefly of failure (v. 19). It is significant, however. The captured cities had been in the mountain area, not in the valley or plain. The plain area referred to is no doubt the flat fertile land running along the Mediterranean. Here the Canaanites used chariots since the flat terrain made it possible. Judah and Simeon, then, had to be content with controlling only the land which was more difficult to farm and was less productive. In general, this was the case with the other tribes too. The better land which was easier to work and more fertile was kept by the former inhabitants while the Israelites were confined to the mountains.

The chariots seemed to constitute the immediate cause of failure. However, in view of the great successes under Joshua and in spite of severe obstacles, the basic cause was certainly the lack of God's blessing. If the people had remained true to Him, no number of iron chariots would have been able to keep Israel from winning their battles.

Today Christians often assign the reason for failures in their lives to immediate obstacles, but the basic reason is the lack of God's blessing due to sin in their lives. God will bless as His children look to Him.

B. The Failure of the Other Tribes (1:21-36)

Here we have the failure of the other tribes in not occupying all their land. The account is brief; but every tribe west of the Jordan (Gad, Reuben and half of Manasseh were east [Num. 32:33]), except Issachar, is listed and its failure registered. The tribe of Issachar may have succeeded in taking all its territory.

First we have some detail regarding the capture of Bethel. It was taken by obtaining information from a man regarding a way into the city. This was probably a way other than the gate which likely was fortified. The city was destroyed, but the man and his family were spared because they had given help. The man then went to "the land of the Hittites" to build another city named Luz. The location is not known. The land of the Hittites itself was far to the north—in the area now occupied by Turkey—and perhaps he went that far. On the other hand the Hittites had also been living in the areas of Palestine for many years (cf. Gen. 23:10; Num. 13:29) and the reference may be to one of these.

Verses 21, 27 and 29-33 list important cities where six of the tribes failed to dislodge the Canaanites. Verse 34 speaks especially of Dan's failure, saying that the former inhabitants forced this tribe totally into the mountains which actually would have been only a small part of the land allotted to the tribe. One note of optimism appears in verse 28 (cf. 30, 33, 35): At a later period when Israel was stronger, the Israelites put the Canaanites under tribute to them.

The overall picture here is one of tragic failure. God had told the people to occupy the land fully, but they did not do so. The other tribes apparently did not even come up to the standard set by Judah and

Simeon, deficient as that was. This was likely because they were unwilling to engage the enemy in combat. This was disobedience on their part. God wanted them to take the land, but they refused to do so. Thus they provided a picture of the disobedience of God's people through all ages.

God calls the Christian to be a soldier in His army. The foe is Satan and his hosts. But too many Christians fail to fight. They are not good soldiers. They disobey their Commander by failing to conquer the enemy territory for Him. What kind of soldiers are we today?

C. Rebuke and Remorse (2:1-5)

1. *Rebuke (2:1-3)*

Because God's people disobeyed, He rebuked them through the "angel of the LORD." Because this angel spoke God's words in the first person, no question exists but that His appearance constituted a theophany, a presentation of God in angel form. Abraham had seen such a theophany at Mamre (Gen. 18), and Joshua had seen one outside Jericho (Josh. 5:13—6:5). Others also had seen them. There is no way to know where this took place in the land. The location is simply called "Bochim" here (meaning "weeping"); and this name was given as a result of this occasion. The rebuke was likely delivered to Israelite leaders assembled in this place.

The angel first reminded the people of God's earlier direction that they make no league with the Canaanites. Of course, they had just done so in letting them remain in the land. He followed this with rebuke because they had disobeyed in this respect, and he asked them the reason. Then he stated that God would let the enemy remain in the land and be "thorns" in their sides to bring constant trouble; and their gods would be a "snare" to them.

A truth should be noted. When Christians insist on their own wrong way, God will often let them go that way so they may see how wrong they are. How much better it is to let God have *His* way. Not only does this please Him, but it is for the believer's good.

2. *Remorse (2:4, 5)*

Those who heard exhibited a good reaction at that time. They showed remorse for their disobedience and wept. They also sacrificed to God. There is no reason to doubt that this was genuine remorse. Those assembled recognized the wrong and repented before God. The following verses show that this attitude did not last long, however. Apparently when the freshness of the rebuke had worn away, it was forgotten. The sinful ways were soon continued, and God found it necessary to take more stringent means of reprimanding His people.

Here, too, a lesson is involved. Remorse and repentance, though sincere at the time, may soon be forgotten. The person may be sincere as these people probably were. But life's realities can quickly blot out that moment from having a lasting effect. Old ways are again pursued, and God is not pleased. He wants the initial remorse, but He also wants a resultant changed life.

II. A General Statement Regarding the Sin of the Period (Judg. 2:6-23)

The remainder of chapter 2 constitutes an introduction to the extensive middle section of the book. The middle section tells of the following periods of oppression and deliverance due to sin. This portion summarizes those periods.

A. Did Well So Long As Joshua's Generation Lived (2:6-9)

The summation begins by telling of the people's condition while Joshua's generation yet lived. The people continued to serve the Lord. One reason is cited: These people "had seen all the great works of the Lord." They had been eyewitnesses of God's great works, such as the opening of the Jordan River at flood stage so the people could cross (Josh. 3:15-17), the toppling of Jericho's walls so the city could be seized (Josh. 6:20) or the prolongation of daylight so the southern confederacy of kings could be defeated (Josh. 10:12-14). Seeing these works, this generation was impressed with God's reality and power and was persuaded to remain faithful to Him.

Recognizing God's greatness regularly serves to keep the Christian faithful. It is when Christians think lightly of God and forget how really powerful He is that they lose out in their spiritual lives. It has been said correctly that the degree of one's true spirituality is proportional to his recognition of God's greatness. The child of God needs to keep this recognition fresh in his mind and heart every day.

A note is needed regarding verse 6. The statement that Joshua "let the people go" probably should not be thought of as an action occurring as a result of the remorse of verses 4 and 5. That time of remorse had followed the failures to take the land, and the failures had come after Joshua had died (cf. 1:1). The statement of 2:6 is parallel with that of Joshua 24:28. Joshua let the people go to occupy their respective inheritances after completing the allotting activity. Verse 6, then, is simply a summary beginning this present portion of the chapter.

Verse 8 gives Joshua's age at his death—110 years. Moses had died when he was 120. Both men likely lived well beyond the average expectancy of the day due to God's gracious blessing and His need for their continued services. Joshua's burial was at Timnath-heres in Ephraim, his home tribe.

B. The Tragic Decline into Sin (2:10-13)

Every generation must make its own choices regarding God. Faithfulness on the part of parents does not insure faithfulness on the part of children. The generation that arose after Joshua's death chose not to follow God. They had not seen God's great works firsthand and evidently were not willing to be impressed with the parents' verbal reports. They had their own ideas and wished to follow them.

One of the great tasks of parents of any day is the rearing of their children. Early training, with stress on God's Word, will do much to direct them aright. Also, parental example which shows the important place of God's Word in their own lives will play a major role. Sometimes the child still goes his own way. He is a person and is responsible to God for himself. However, the parent should count it a prime task in life to do all that is possible in leading and counseling him so he will truly follow the Lord. Much time should be spent praying to that end.

For the generation following Joshua the big attraction away from God was the worship of Baal. Verse 11 says they "served Baalim." The plural form of *Baal* is here used to designate the many local representations of Baal. Thus the Scriptures speak of the god Baal-peor (Num. 25:3, 5), Baal-zebub (2 Kings 1:2, 3, 6), *et al.* Many cities of the Canaanites had their local Baals, but all Baals were essentially the main god Baal. Then verse 13 speaks of both "Baal and Ashtaroth." The latter was a goddess, the patroness of love and war. Worship of her regularly accompanied worship of Baal, and it was highly licentious. As noted previously, the Israelites' attraction toward this worship was mainly materialistic. They wanted good crops; and they believed that Baal, the alleged god of rainfall, could insure this. This was a grave error, however. Only the true God could do this.

Today people act just as foolishly when they put materialistic gain ahead of devotion to God. Unsaved people may refuse Christ because they believe they will lose out in business, not being able to continue former wrong practices. Christians may refuse to take a church office or attend services regularly because they want to pursue their own material profit and pleasure. But true benefit for this life and the next is found in giving oneself fully to God.

C. Chastisement from God (2:14, 15, 20-23)

God is gracious and long-suffering as He waits for His people to turn to Him. But in His time He speaks; and then it is in harsh tones. He did so here. God's anger became "hot against Israel"; He delivered them to "spoilers" and "sold them into the hands of their enemies." These "spoilers" and "enemies" were the various oppressing nations as set forth in following chapters of the book. Here we have the indication of what God would do, and the succeeding chapters tell of this being done. Verse 15 is particularly sad. We see that God's hand came "against them for evil." God wants to be *for* His people, but sin prevents this. God permitted these enemies to come against Israel, and He didn't bring resistance to counter them.

Verses 20-23 speak of another way God chastised them. It is the same as that mentioned by the angel of the Lord in 2:3. Not only would God permit outside nations to come against Israel, but He would let the Canaanites who were already in the land continue to live there. They would cause trouble for Israel by being a bad influence on them and keeping them confined geographically to the mountains. This was a part of the discipline the Israelites needed.

D. The Provision of Judges (2:16-19)

Here we see God's gracious provision in the judges. Judges were raised up to deliver the people from the oppressing nations. God might have left the people in their desperate situation without giving this manner of help, but He did not. He gave them these deliverers. There were twelve of these judges, ending with Samson. Not all began by effecting a military deliverance, but many did. These would first lead an Israelite army in victory against the oppressing nation; then they would continue in a supervisory position over the people. They were not elected to office; neither were they entitled "king" or "governor." God caused the people to recognize them, however, thus leading to helpful supervision and the restraint of sin. Actually the term by which they came to be called—"judges"—has its significance primarily in their work as supervisors, rather than as military deliverers.

Verse 17 states that the people wouldn't listen to the judges' admonitions but went after false gods. Some people listened, and the situation was better; but many did not. Nevertheless, God still delivered through these leaders (v. 18). Verse 19 adds the tragic note that when a particular judge had died, the people would again revert to former ways and even worse. This indicates that as long as a judge lived, improvement in the people's conduct was experienced; but when he died, they became yet more sinful. The average trend was continually downward.

This testifies to the wickedness of the human heart. God was displeased with the people in that day, and He is today when people persist in their wicked ways.

Prepare To Answer Intelligently

1. What tribe was designated to go first against the Canaanites?
2. Why was it logical for this tribe to ask Simeon to help?
3. Was Jerusalem captured permanently at this time?
4. What type of land did the tribes capture?
5. Whom did God send to rebuke the people for their failure?
6. What was the reaction to this rebuke?
7. What major factor kept Israel serving God as long as Joshua's generation lived?
8. What tragic change came with the generation after Joshua?
9. What two things did God say He would do to bring chastisement?
10. What was the work of the judges?

CHAPTER 3

The First Two Oppressions

BIBLE PORTION TO READ: Judges 3:1-31

IN CHAPTER 3 of the Book of Judges the record of the oppressions and deliverances begins. Two cycles of these oppressions and deliverances are presented. In the first the oppressing nation was from Mesopotamia, and the deliverer was Othniel. In the second the nation was Moab and the deliverer, Ehud. Before setting forth these two cycles, however, the chapter has more to say regarding the people's sin.

I. Dwelling with the Canaanites (Judg. 3:1-7)

The general section of the chapter sets forth three matters especially. It speaks further of God's reason for permitting foreign groups to remain in the land; it identifies these groups; and it tells of Israel's sin in becoming involved with these groups.

A. Reasons for Permitting Foreign Groups To Remain (3:1, 2, 4)

Further explanation (cf. 2:3, 22) was here given regarding God's reasons for permitting foreign groups to live in the land with the Israelites. The tribes had been wrong in not driving out these groups completely as God had commanded; but since they had not, there were reasons for allowing them to remain. Two reasons are cited:

1. *The First Reason (3:1, 2)*
The first reason was so the people could learn that warfare—or any other activity for God—is accomplished only when one looks to God for help. The following understanding of verses 1 and 2 reveals this thought. In verse 1 we have the statement that the nations—soon to be identified in verses 3 and 5—were left in the land "to prove" or test the Israelites. These Israelites were the next generation (after Joshua) who "had not known all the wars of Canaan." Then verse 2 states that God wanted this generation to learn—as a result of these groups being there—how to make war. That is, through these groups God would "teach them war." On the surface this sounds strange, but the thought is clear. This new generation had not seen God make war through their fathers. Therefore, God would teach them how to make war for Him. They were not to trust in large armies or powerful weapons but in God. The neighboring nations made war in the normal way, but God's people were to make it by trusting Him.

The earlier generation had learned this; and because they had, they had experienced great victories. When they had come to Jericho with its walls impossible to storm, they had followed God's way of bringing down the walls by marching around the city (Josh. 6:20). When they had needed to catch and defeat Canaanite kings, they had trusted God to prolong a day (Josh. 10:12-14). Their victories had been accomplished by God's help, not through numbers or weapons. One of the greatest truths set forth in Scripture is that God's people experience victory only when they trust Him. Defeat comes when they don't. This truth is vital for every Christian to know and keep in mind at all times.

2. *The Second Reason (3:4)*
The second reason is that these remaining groups would provide a test to determine whether or not the Israelites would choose to obey God. These people, with their pagan ways of worship, would be a continual challenge to the Israelites to show whether they

would remain faithful to God or be influenced to follow pagan ways.

Note these two truths: First, it is better for God's people to carry out God's will from the first. That is, they should not let the foreign groups remain in the land as Israel did. Israel's later experience in the land would have been much easier if the groups had been driven out as God had directed. Second, at times God permits matters to come into the lives of His children which test them. These tests give the Christian opportunity to show whether or not he will choose for God. To choose aright, in spite of the attractions such tests present, makes the choice of high value in God's sight. If Israel had proved true to God and resisted the influence of these remaining groups in this instance, their obedience would have been of high value. However, as the Book of Judges so clearly shows, they did not resist. Instead, they were greatly influenced and sinned grievously before God.

B. Identity of the Foreign Groups (3:3, 5)

The foreign groups are identified in two ways—by locality where they lived and by nationality.

1. *According to Locality (3:3)*

The thoughts presented in verse 3 are essentially the same as in Joshua 13:2-6 where greater detail was given. The "five lords of the Philistines" are identified as the rulers over Gaza, Ashdod, Ashkelon, Gath and Ekron (Josh. 13:3). These were the five main cities of the Philistines, and their respective rulers served as a sort of five-member committee to govern the land (cf. 1 Sam. 5:8, 11; 6:4, 16, 17). The passage also indicates the extent of the land referred to. It stretched from Sihor (present El Arish) in the south to Ekron in the north. Ekron was the northernmost of the five Philistine cities, just slightly north of the latitudinal parallel of Jerusalem. The latter part of verse 3 (corresponding to Joshua 13:4-6) refers to the inhabitants of the north.

The region in mind includes both the coastal region, extending from Aphek (near Ekron) north to Sidon (Phoenician capital), and the inland region near Mount Hermon (Mount Lebanon) and north to the approach to Hamath. In summary, the land not taken by the tribes was the entire coastal territory from south of the Israelite land to the far north and then all the northern territory. The former inhabitants were permitted to remain in these territories.

Some cities listed in last week's lesson as not captured by the tribes (cf. Judg. 1:21, 27, 29-33) were located in places not included in these territories. The reason for their not being listed here seems to be that the intent is to designate whole geographic territories not captured rather than individual cities. The total area not captured included the large geographical territories set forth here plus the cities listed in chapter 1.

2. *According to Nationality (3:5)*

Verse 5 lists six nations or tribes as constituting the people left in these territories; namely the Canaanites, Hittites, Amorites, Perizzites, Hivites and Jebusites. This same listing of nations occurs a few other times (cf. Exod. 3:8, 17; 23:23; 33:2; Deut. 20:17). Other times the listing includes a seventh, the Girgashites (cf. Deut. 7:1; Josh. 3:10; 24:11). Perhaps the Girgashites were a smaller group and so were left out of the other listings. In the light of Genesis 10:15-18, these nations could properly be thought of as divisions of Canaanites. That is, though the Canaanites could be listed as one of these nations in a limited sense, in a broader sense they could be thought of as including them. Put another way, these nations which constituted the population of Palestine at the time of Joshua's conquest were subdivisions of the Canaanite family. At least some of these subdivisions (e.g., the Amorites and Hittites) represent early migrations into the land. The people intermarried with the Canaanites living there and became subdivisions of them.

C. The Sin with These Foreign Groups (3:6, 7)

Note two aspects of the Israelites' sin as it relates to these foreign groups in chapter 2:

1. *Intermarriage (3:6)*

The first sin was that of intermarriage. God had warned specifically against this sin (cf. Exod. 34:15, 16; Deut. 7:3, 4). A chief reason He had wanted the Israelites to drive out the Canaanites was to avoid this sin. Living close together in the land, it was quite inevitable that they would intermarry.

The wrong was twofold. Intermarriage contributed significantly to Israel's changing to the worship of Baal. Being married to Baal worshipers made the influence to worship him much greater. A second wrong was that if intermarriage became common, the identity of the Israelites would be endangered. God had been careful that Israel's identity be maintained while developing into the status of a nation. He did not want it jeopardized at this stage of their history.

2. *Worship of Baal (3:7)*

The second matter set forth in chapter 2 was the worship of Baal (2:11, 13). The word translated "groves" in the King James Version is better simply transliterated as *Asheroth*. It refers to the Canaanite goddess Asherah, Baal's consort. This goddess was worshiped along with Ashtaroth (2:13), and worship to her was as licentious as that to Ashtaroth. Lewdly carved poles were erected in her honor near Baal altars (cf. Judg. 6:25). This Baal-centered religion was very offensive to God, and the tribes' sin in pursuing it was great in His sight.

II. The Mesopotamian Oppression and Deliverance (Judg. 3:8-11)

Here we have the beginning of the accounts of the cycles of oppression and deliverance which occurred because of the people's sin. Verse 8 says specifically that this first one came because "the anger of the LORD was hot against Israel."

A. The Oppression of the Mesopotamians (3:8)

The first oppressors were the Mesopotamians under the leadership of Chushan-rishathaim. Mesopotamia was the farthest removed of any nation which oppressed Israel. For some reason Chushan-rishathaim had campaigned far from home in effecting this conquest of Palestine. We don't know how he carried it out or how many tribes he controlled. Only the duration is given: eight years. Toward the close of this period the people began to cry to God for relief; and God gave it through Othniel, Caleb's nephew.

B. The Deliverance of Othniel (13:9-11)

1. *Raised Up by God (3:9)*

Previously we noted that Othniel made conquest of Debir (Judg. 1:11-15; Josh. 15:15-19). Now God used him to deliver Israel from these Mesopotamians. Verse 9 states that God raised him up for this task. This means that God brought about circumstances that led to his taking the lead in effecting the deliverance. He had been prepared beforehand. No doubt the conquest of Debir played a role in that preparation. Now God ordered events to bring about this result.

God superintends history. Sometimes it is difficult to see how God's plan is being effected, but we know it is. Often it seems a leader is needed to take charge. When such a one doesn't appear, the Christian may wonder if God is carrying out His plan. But in His own time and way, God raises up those needed to lead in days of crisis. God knows and will always do that which is best. Those whom God would have step into places of leadership must respond when He calls.

Notice further that it was only when "the children of Israel cried unto the LORD" that God intervened. Sin withholds God's blessing. True repentance brings the desired relief. In the Christian's life blessing will come when God sees he has a repentant heart. The person without God's blessing must turn to Him in humility, and God will respond graciously. The same applies in the life of a church. Sin in people's lives will withhold God's blessing.

2. *Enabled by the Holy Spirit (3:10)*

Note verse 10 particularly. Othniel was enabled to do this work for God when the "Spirit of the LORD" came on him. He then "judged Israel, and went out to war." The result was victory over the oppressing foe. In future lessons we will see that three other judges experienced the Spirit's coming on them (Gideon, Judg. 6:34; Jephthah, Judg. 11:29; and Samson, Judg. 13:25; 14:6, 19; 15:14). The purpose in each case was to enable the person to do the work God assigned. The Holy Spirit, the third Person of the Godhead, gave these people ability and strength beyond that which was normal for them so they could do the work.

The Holy Spirit does the same today. He enters the life of the Christian at the time of salvation and enables that one for God-assigned tasks. The person may believe he is incapable of teaching a Sunday School class, but the Holy Spirit will give that ability. The young person may believe that he cannot become a pastor or missionary; therefore, he rejects the call to such a ministry. Again the Holy Spirit will grant the necessary ability. If God calls, He makes provision if one responds to the call and trusts God.

3. *Rest in the Land (3:11)*

Othniel defeated the enemy; then the land "had rest forty years." The fact that the statement about Othniel's death comes only ofter this mention of the land having rest suggests that Othniel lived these forty years. If so, he likely judged Israel most of this time. The fact that the land had rest for this period was undoubtedly due to sin's curtailment which was due in part to Othniel's work. As he grew old, his influence waned and sin again became flagrant. This led to the second period of oppression.

III. The Moabite Oppression and Deliverance (Judg. 3:12-31)

A. The Oppression of the Moabites (3:12-14)

The second oppressing nation was located nearer to Israel. Moab lay across the Dead Sea from the tribe of Judah. In order to enter Palestine, the Moabites merely had to cross the Jordan just north of the Dead Sea. Then they would arrive in the area of Jericho. God allowed this oppressing enemy to come because Israel "had done evil in the sight of the LORD" (3:12). In this endeavor the Moabites had help from two nearby nations, the Ammonites and Amalekites (3:13). Eglon was the Moabite king who led in the conquest, and he controlled Israel for eighteen years. He made Jericho his center of operations. He likely didn't control all the tribal areas but only the land around Jericho. This probably included a part of the tribes of Judah, Benjamin and Ephraim.

B. The Deliverance of Ehud (3:15-30)

This time God chose a left-handed Benjamite named Ehud to bring deliverance (3:15).

1. *The Unusual Manner of This Deliverance (3:15-30)*

The way God led Ehud to deliver Israel this time was different from the other instances. He didn't lead an army to attack Eglon's forces. Rather, he entered the palace of the enemy king, slew him with a dagger, withdrew quietly without raising an alarm and then led the people to kill the Moabites as they tried to move homeward without a leader.

Ehud brought a present from the Israelites to Eglon. The proud king was willing to accept this. Before Ehud went to Eglon, he secreted an eighteen-inch, double-edged dagger on his thigh. He and his party gained admittance to the king, and he presented the gift. Ehud and his party then left and went as far as Gilgal near Jericho. Here he left his party and returned alone to the palace, telling Eglon that he had a secret "message from God" for him. After the servants left the room where the two met, Ehud grasped the dagger from his thigh and plunged it into the fat king's midsection. The flesh completely enclosed the weapon, and Ehud left it there. Eglon died as Ehud quietly left the room, locked the doors and quickly left the palace. He was safely away before servants opened the room, finding the dead body. Ehud called the Israelites to go with him to the Jordan to control the fords, intercepting the returning Moabites. Many Israelites responded, and some 10,000 of the enemy were killed, ending Moabite domination.

2. *Lessons To Notice*

One person can do much for God if he is fully dedicated. Sometimes we think that nothing effective can be accomplished unless many are involved. However, Ehud effected this deliverance for Israel almost singlehandedly. He planned how he could accomplish the task by himself; then he carried it out. The plan involved trickery, and Ehud has been criticized for this. But he did accomplish his goal. In so doing he displayed what one man can do. God might have used a higher means had Ehud sought His direction, but this was likely a common strategy of the time.

Another lesson to notice concerns Ehud's great courage. The plan he devised was very dangerous. He might have been stopped even before he started if he had let his mind dwell on the dangers. A timid man—or one who did not have real faith in God's help—would not have let himself think of such a plan, much less carry it out. But Ehud formulated the plan, saw that it had definite possibilities of success and proceeded with it. Great faith was demanded at every step.

Christians need to exercise similar faith and courage as they serve God today. Many fear what may happen —even in the way of personal embarrassment—if they venture for the Savior.

We can learn another lesson from the readiness of others to join Ehud to control the fords of the Jordan. Perhaps Ehud's personal boldness finally aroused them. Today in Christian work one person's leadership is needed to arouse others. But even with such leadership some refuse to respond. However, God is pleased when many give themselves for the task.

C. Shamgar, the Third Judge (3:31)

The last verse of the chapter speaks of Ehud's successor. Shamgar was one of the twelve, but not one of the six who brought deliverance from oppressing nations. However, he "slew of the Philistines six hundred men with an ox goad: and he also delivered Israel." This feat probably occurred when a Philistine force invaded the land and he was able to drive the enemy back by himself. This was a tremendous feat. It doesn't necessarily mean that all six hundred were killed in a single encounter. This was a great exploit. We don't know whether Shamgar continued to serve as judge after this.

Prepare To Answer Intelligently

1. What was one reason for permitting foreign groups to live in the land?
2. What was the second reason?
3. Where did these groups live?
4. Of what six nations were they composed?
5. What two main sins did Israel commit as a result of these groups living in the land?
6. Who was the leader of the Mesopotamians?
7. Who did God choose to deliver Israel from the Mesopotamians?
8. What was the importance of the Holy Spirit's coming on this man?
9. Who did God choose to deliver Israel from the Moabites?
10. How did this man kill the king of the Moabites?
11. What was it that this man wanted others to help him do at the Jordan?

CHAPTER 4

Deborah and Barak Against Sisera

BIBLE PORTION TO READ: Judges 4:1—5:31

THE THIRD CYCLE of oppression and deliverance is the subject of this lesson. Greater detail is given than with either of the first two cycles. The history is set forth in chapter 4, and a song which Deborah composed for the occasion (cf. 5:3, 7) is recorded in chapter 5. The lesson material does not discuss the song as such, but information from it is noted as it bears on the history from chapter 4.

I. The Oppression of the Canaanites (Judg. 4:1-3)

A. Identity of the Oppressor (4:1, 2)

1. *Canaanites*

This time the oppressing people were the Canaanites who had been allowed to continue living in the land. By the time of this lesson approximately a century and a half had elapsed since Joshua's death. During this time these Canaanites had apparently remained quiet and had not attempted any retaliation. They had permitted the Israelites to live in the mountainous areas without trying to drive them out of the area which was formerly theirs. Now, however, the Canaanites did attempt to retaliate; and they succeeded in bringing the Israelites under their control.

2. *Jabin, King of the Canaanites*

The leader of this uprising was Jabin, king in Hazor. Hazor was located in the far north, near Lake Huleh above the Sea of Galilee. It was in the tribal area of Naphtali, but clearly it had never been occupied by Naphtali. It had been the center of the earlier struggle when Joshua had defeated the northern confederacy (Josh. 11:1-14). At that time also the king of Hazor was called Jabin although certainly he was another man, likely an ancestor of the ruler mentioned here. Hazor has been identified and excavated and would have been considered a metropolis in its day. Whereas most cities of the time averaged only eight to fifteen acres in size, Hazor covered no less than two hundred. It was no wonder that it was the leading city in Joshua's day as well as in Deborah's and Barak's. Because the city was far north, however, it is likely that this Canaanite uprising involved only the northern tribes.

3. *Sisera, the General*

Jabin himself did not do the fighting. He had a skilled military leader, Sisera, with headquarters in Harosheth. Harosheth is believed to be the present Tell el-Harbaj, a six-acre site on the south bank of the Kishon River at the foot of Mount Carmel. If this is correct, Harosheth was something more than thirty miles southwest of Hazor where Jabin ruled, and it was located in the fine Esdraelon Valley. Sisera had gained control over the Israelites of the area by using nine hundred chariots of iron. Chariots had also been used years before to withstand the advances of Judah and Simeon in the southwest (Judg. 1:19). This form of weapon was especially effective in level valleys, and the Esdraelon was quite suitable.

B. The Severity of the Oppression (4:3)

Sisera continued his control over the Israelites for twenty years, longer than any of the oppressing nations except the Philistines. The hardship imposed is described with the strong term "mightily oppressed" (Hebrew:

"he squeezed with strength"). This caused the Israelites to cry "unto the LORD" for relief; and as before, God heard and raised up those to bring deliverance.

The increase in the oppression's length and severity suggests that Israel's sin had been getting progressively worse with God permitting more severe reprisal. God does suit punishment to the seriousness of the sin. There will apparently be degrees of punishment even in the eternal state of Hell (cf. Matt. 11:20-24).

II. The Deliverers (Judg. 4:4-9)

A. Deborah, a Prophetess

This time God employed two people to lead in the deliverance. One was a woman named Deborah, the wife of Lapidoth. She is called a prophetess, meaning that God had communicated His word to her to give to the Israelites. She also had already been serving as a judge. She was unique in this, for other judges earned this status through their military deliverances. However, people were already coming to her, apparently sharing their problems and hearing her solutions as she sat under a palm tree "between Ramah and Bethel" in the tribe of Benjamin. Clearly Deborah was not an ordinary woman. She had outstanding ability and evidently was truly devoted to God.

God's work always has a great need for people who are able and dedicated. The dedication is more important than the ability; but the most effective service can be rendered when both exist. Sometimes Christian parents with gifted children think these children should go only into a secular occupation where their talents can "really" be used. This is wrong thinking. God's work calls for the best, and no person should think that talents cannot or will not be used to their fullest degree there. No area of work requires greater need for ability or provides more significant satisfaction in meeting that need than does the service of God.

B. Barak

The man was named Barak. He did not live near

Deborah but in the north—in the midst of the area where Jabin and Sisera held control over the Israelites. His hometown was Kedesh in Naphtali, identified with present-day Tell Qades, within sight of Hazor, Jabin's capital. He became involved when Deborah asked him to lead against Sisera. The task of finding a leader fell to her because of her recognized leadership in the land. She properly recognized that she, a woman, should not assume the military leadership herself. This led her to ask Barak. We do not know why she chose him, but probably he already had some reputation as a leader with military prowess. His living where the domination existed could have been a factor too.

Deborah requested that Barak assemble 10,000 men as soldiers from the two northern tribes, Zebulun and Naphtali, and then move with them to Mount Tabor where he could join battle with Sisera. Barak agreed, providing that Deborah would work with him. She said she would, but Barak should know that his effort would not work to his own honor but to that of a woman. She was not referring to herself but to one into whose hand God would deliver Sisera in due time (4:17-22).

It is not clear why Barak insisted on Deborah's help. Surely he was a capable leader. He seems to have lacked courage and wanted the support of one who had already demonstrated strength and faith in God. Sometimes today's Christians lack the courage to move out alone in God's work and need the support of others. They may be criticized for not having the courage, but at least they can be commended for acting when encouragement is given. Many Christians do nothing at all even when they are encouraged by others.

We must admire Deborah for giving encouragement. She could have objected to Barak's request and tried to shame him into going alone. Or she could have refused to comply with his request, arguing that the request was wrong. Often Christians assert their alleged rights even though the Lord's work suffers. Deborah might have insisted on hers; but if she had, it is unlikely that the

Canaanites would have been defeated. The blame would have been mainly Barak's, but still Israel would not have been delivered. Deborah realized that this was the important issue—not whether or not some of her rights would be violated.

III. Battle and Victory (Judg. 4:10-16; 5:14-23)
A. The Setting (4:10-13; 5:14-18)
1. *Israel's Preparation (4:10; 5:14-18)*

Here we have the setting for the battle, beginning with Israel's preparation for it. In 4:10 we see that Barak carried out Deborah's directive in assembling the 10,000 soldiers. These came primarily from the tribes of Zebulun and Naphtali. He gathered them at Kedesh where Deborah met him; then he moved with them to Mount Tabor. That these men were "at his feet" (4:10) shows they submitted to his leadership. They must have respected Barak. After Barak and Deborah met, they undoubtedly counseled together regarding the plan of attack. God's work calls for wise procedures which come from counseling together.

In Deborah's song we find further information regarding those who responded to Barak's call (5:14-18). The tribes who responded were Ephraim, Benjamin, Machir (meaning the one-half of Manasseh on the west of the Jordan near Ephraim), Zebulun and Issachar (vv. 14, 15). But verse 18 emphasizes that the major number of men came from Zebulun and Naphtali, stating that those from these tribes "jeoparded their lives unto the death." This apparently meant that these came in greater number and fought harder. The overall thought must be that some volunteers came from the other tribes listed, but the greater number came from the two. Perhaps this should have been expected since the tribal areas of these two were probably the most affected by the oppression.

Then 5:15b-17 lists tribes that did not take part. Reuben is said to have had "great thoughts of heart" concerning the need but did not send people. Gilead, meaning the other half of Manasseh, continued to abide "beyond Jordan" on the east. Dan yet remained "in ships," meaning that this tribe did not interrupt its normal trading activities to go to war. "Asher continued on the sea shore" and remained quite undisturbed by the need of the hour. Three tribes are not mentioned at all: Judah, Simeon and Gad. These three were far away from the area of oppression which gave them some excuse. Reuben was also far away, but it is at least said to its credit that its people shared in "thoughts of heart." Real blame must be laid at the feet of Dan, Gilead and Asher, however. They were nearby but did not get involved.

Many Christians are like these negligent tribes. They wish to have others do the work. But God is not pleased with this attitude. Every Christian should be ready to give himself.

2. *The Kenites (4:11)*

As a means of understanding what develops in the latter part of the chapter, a word is included regarding the Kenites who lived at Zaanaim in the region of Barak's hometown. Heber, a Kenite and descendant of Moses' father-in-law, had settled in this place; and Jael, to whom Sisera was shortly to come in flight, was his wife.

3. *Sisera's Preparation (4:12, 13)*

Sisera heard of Israel's preparation for war. He gathered his nine hundred chariots and men of war and brought them from Harosheth to the valley of the Kishon River. The Kishon still flows through the Esdraelon Valley near the foot of the Carmel range of mountains. It flows near ancient Harosheth. Thus Sisera did not have to move his troops very far to reach the battlefield that he had chosen.

B. The Battle (4:14)

1. *Encouragement of Deborah (4:14)*

Although Barak, being a male, was the one who actually led the army into battle, Deborah provided the needed encouragement. She had responded to his earlier request by helping make plans. Now she encouraged him to move into battle. Today those who "hold the ropes" for those who move into battle for God are important. Christians at home can do much by praying for missionaries on the field.

2. *Deborah's Encouragement Was God-centered (4:14)*

Note Deborah's manner of encouraging Barak. She didn't tell him to have courage because of his army of ten thousand men. Probably Sisera's army was yet larger; and Sisera had nine hundred chariots besides, giving him an advantage. No doubt Sisera relied heavily on these for fighting in the level Esdraelon Valley.

Deborah's encouragement was in God. Victory for Barak would depend on God's blessing (4:14).

Numbers of people have their place, and skill is important in doing God's work; but the difference between victory and defeat depends on God's blessing. With blessing, victory is achieved; without blessing, defeat is experienced.

3. *Barak Waged an Offensive Battle (4:14)*

Barak didn't wait for Sisera to attack but took the offensive against him. He met the enemy near the Kishon River "by the waters of Megiddo" (5:19). His willingness to attack shows his confidence in God.

Too often Christians hesitate and wait for the enemy to attack them. But when one is always on the defensive, he tends to give ground. The Christian has the truth and should have the courage and confidence in God to take the offensive.

C. The Victory (4:15, 16; 5:19-23)

1. *Defeat of the Enemy Army*

The emphasis of the account is significantly on what God did, not what Barak did. The text states that "the LORD discomfited Sisera"; so Barak defeated him with "the edge of the sword." Barak's men were not really the ones who gained the victory. Rather, God won it through using swords in the hands of men.

Deborah's song (5:19-22) indicates how God effected the victory. In addition to enabling the sword-wielding men, He employed the weather, causing much rain to fall; for the indication is that the "river of Kishon swept" away Sisera's forces. Sisera wanted to fight the battle on the plain since he could use his prized chariots. But the opposite was true. The shallow Kishon overflowed because of the rain, hindering the chariots. They became mired in the water and mud. We read, too, that "the horsehoofs were broken by the means of the pransings." This likely means that the horses pulling the chariots broke ranks as the chariots became mired and galloped away, leaving them behind. This put the enemy in complete disarray. Barak's troops harrassed them at will and pursued them as they fled. How easily God can effect victory for His people if they proceed when, how and as He directs.

In 5:23 the inhabitants of Meroz were cursed for not coming "to the help of the Lord." Meroz was a city located in the vicinity whose inhabitants could have helped significantly in the battle. Perhaps their position gave them an advantage for attacking the Canaanites during this flight. However, they chose not to become involved.

Christians should be ready to become involved in God's work. Satanic hosts are continually endeavoring to hinder God's work; but God expects His own to serve as good soldiers in the war against Satan.

2. *Flight of Sisera*

While the enemy was routed, Sisera himself also fled. However, he apparently went alone, trying to get to Jabin in Hazor. Perhaps he wished to report on what had just happened so it would be presented in the best possible light. His not remaining with his army but taking this different route would not have helped maintain order among his troops. Perhaps he saw that things were about as bad as they could be. Therefore, he believed that no greater harm would be done by leaving.

IV. The Courage of Jael the Kenite (Judg. 4:17-22; 5:24-27)

A. The Story

Sisera did not get as far as Hazor before he felt too exhausted to continue. He stopped at the tent of Heber the Kenite. Probably he intended to rest for a time and then move on. Peace apparently existed between Heber and Jabin (4:17). Heber probably wasn't home at the time, for his wife Jael met Sisera, invited him into the tent and gave him provisions (4:18, 19; 5:25). Then he laid down for the needed rest; but before falling asleep, he asked her to turn away from the tent any who might be looking for him. After Sisera fell asleep, Jael took a tent peg and hammer, driving the tent peg through Sisera's temple into the ground, pinning him where he lay. Barak arrived shortly after, and Jael showed him his dead enemy. Since Sisera was dead, Barak did not have the satisfaction of killing him. This confirmed Deborah's earlier statement—that because he refused to go against the Canaanites alone, the victory would be for the honor of a woman (4:9). This woman was Jael.

B. The Lesson

The principle lesson from Jael's action concerns courage. Those who fight God's battles are to display courage. Sisera was a strong and feared man of war and Jael a mere woman; yet she took his life. This took an unusual degree of bravery and courage. God highly honored her for her courage (Judg. 5:24).

We don't know why Jael chose to kill Sisera this way. She showed courage, but was she right in what she did—first in being kind to the person and then killing him? Maybe she wasn't acting deceitfully in her initial kindness. She may not have known of his defeat. He apparently had come directly from the battle scene; therefore, she hadn't heard the news. Jael's kindness, too, may have been due to the peace existing between her family and Jabin. If this is correct, her first inkling of what had happened could have come only after Sisera had entered the tent and she had served him. When he told her to keep out any pursuers, she probably wanted to know why. Therefore, the weary general may have fallen asleep before Jael faced the decision of what to do. Should she kill this man, thus siding with Israel with whom ties of history had been made in Moses? Or should she protect him and continue the peace arrangements with the Canaanites? She sided with Israel. This took great courage.

V. Relief from Canaanite Oppression (Judg. 4:23, 24)

The result of Barak's victory and Jael's courage was full relief from Canaanite oppression for Israel. Verse 24 states that "the children of Israel" prevailed against Jabin until they destroyed him. Not only had Israel been delivered from him, but he was finally killed. We don't know how it took place, but Jabin's killing completed Israel's deliverance.

The overall story presents a picture of what results when God's people trust Him as Deborah and Barak did. They made their plan and pressed the attack, depending on God, not themselves. When Christians move out for God in this way, victory is assured.

Prepare To Answer Intelligently

1. Where did Jabin live? Where did Sisera live?
2. What was Sisera's main offensive weapon?
3. Where did Deborah serve as a judge in Israel?
4. Where did Barak live in reference to Deborah?
5. Where did these two assemble their troops?
6. What tribes sent troops for Barak's army?
7. Where was the battle with Sisera fought?
8. How did God bring victory to Barak's troops?
9. Who received Sisera into her tent?
10. How did she take Sisera's life?

CHAPTER 5

The Man Gideon

BIBLE PORTION TO READ: Judges 6:1-40

THE FOURTH OPPRESSION of the Israelites came from the Midianites who lived northeast of the Moabites on the east of the Jordan. This time the deliverer God used was Gideon, of whom more is recorded than of any other judge. Because God saw enough significance in his life to place this much emphasis on it, we will appropriately spend more than one lesson studying about him. This lesson covers only the first of the three chapters recording his exploits.

I. The Midianite Oppression (Judg. 6:1-10)

A. Character of the Oppression (6:1-6)

1. *The Oppressors (6:1-3)*

This time the oppressing enemy was composed mainly of Midianites who were distantly related to the Israelites, being descendants of Abraham by Keturah (Gen. 25:2). However, they had assistance from two other groups, the Amalekites and "the children of the east." This last group was very likely composed of people of different backgrounds who hoped to gain some spoil for themselves.

2. *The Oppression (6:4-6)*

This Midianite oppression seems to have been one of the most humiliating of all for Israel. Verse 3 suggests that the enemy came annually to seize the year's harvest. Apparently the Israelites would do the work, but the enemy would appear in time to take the crop. They likely kept a residual force in the land in order to keep matters under control, and they brought the main group in only once a year.

When the large group of Midianites came, they seized what they wanted, including animals as well as grain (v. 4). They came in large numbers, like "grasshoppers for multitude" (v. 5); and they "greatly impoverished" the Israelites (v. 6). They came primarily to the productive Esdraelon valley which ran on an angle from the Mediterranean Sea all the way to the Jordan valley. Verse 4 states that they also turned south from the Esdraelon valley as far as Gaza. This would have involved the level terrain along the Mediterranean which was also good for growing grain. The Midianites knew where to find the best grain and other produce. The Israelites feared the enemy greatly, hiding both themselves and their produce in caves (v. 2). This continued for seven years (v. 1).

This is a shameful, sad picture of God's people. They had enjoyed such promise of better things in the days of Moses and Joshua, but now they had come to this condition of abject humiliation. This is a telling lesson of what sin can do to people. Let every Christian person and organization take warning.

B. Admonition by a Prophet (6:7-10)

When the people once more called to God for relief, He heard them. However, His first response was not to send Gideon but "a prophet." We do not have the man's name, but his availability shows that prophets lived and served during the Period of the Judges. His message was twofold: First, to remind the people of God's goodness in bringing them from Egypt and causing them to make conquest of Canaan (vv. 8, 9); and second, to reprimand them for not obeying the Lord Who had told them not to fear the former inhabitants (v. 10). Remembering God's past goodness is one way

God uses to prompt His people to obey Him in the present. The prophet spoke of the people's disobedience as the reason God had permitted the oppression to come. Apparently God sent the prophet to the people so that Gideon's work and ministry would be more effective.

II. The Call of Gideon (Judg. 6:11-24)

A. The Call Proper (6:11-16)

1. *The Angel of the Lord (6:11, 12)*

When God called Gideon, He did so through the "angel of the LORD." This One was the Second Person of the Trinity in a temporary human form. He had likewise assumed a human body in appearing to Abraham at Mamre (Gen. 18), to Joshua outside Jericho (Josh. 5:13—6:5) and to others (cf. Gen. 16:7-13; Exod. 3:2-6; Num. 22:22-35; Judg. 13:3-22). Since God extended the call through the Angel, we can see the importance He placed on it. Few through the ages have been so honored.

The Angel came to Gideon as Gideon "threshed wheat by the winepress, to hide it from the Midianites." The winepress was not an ordinary place to thresh wheat, but evidently it was safer at this time. The Angel must have appeared as an ordinary wayfarer. First He seated Himself under a tree as if to enjoy a little shade; then He extended the call to Gideon.

2. *A Significant Interchange of Words (6:13-16)*

The Angel began by stating, "The LORD is with thee, thou mighty man of valour." The words seem out of place in view of Gideon's immediate response. Gideon asked why all the difficulties had befallen the people if God was with them. Why hadn't God wrought miracles to bring deliverance as He had done in Egypt? Such words don't seem to indicate that their speaker was a "mighty man of valour." That Gideon's words weren't really characteristic of him, however, is clarified by the Angel's next words. He ignored Gideon's words and proceeded to tell him God was calling him to service. Gideon was to "go" in His might, and He would "save Israel from the hand of the Midianites." Gideon then indicated how humble he was as he emphasized his and his family's lowly position. However, the Angel told Gideon that he would be able to "smite the Midianites as one man" because God Himself would be with him.

This conversation is significant both as it shows the kind of person Gideon really was and God's wisdom and tenderness in calling him. The overall story shows that Gideon was truly a "mighty man of valour" as the Angel had stated. Therefore, we must understand Gideon's response as an outburst from a breaking heart rather than a revelation of his true character. God would neither have called him nor spoken to him as He did here if the case had been otherwise.

Gideon lived in a different day. Apparently all his hometown of Ophrah (located somewhere in the Esdraelon valley) had adopted Baal worship. As we will see later, he quite clearly had stood almost alone against this tide of change, and six years had passed with no apparent answer to his prayer for deliverance. Now that this message from God had come to him, the pent-up emotions broke forth and he spoke the words of complaint.

We see God's tenderness and understanding in the Angel's reply. He didn't rebuke Gideon but simply extended the call and encouraged him. Notice that He stressed the reason that victory would be certain: God would be with Gideon.

God knows all and is gracious. He knew Gideon's true heart and how best to extend the call. God knows the hearts of all His children. He knows when rebuke is deserved; He also knows when there have been long trial and years of praying without an apparent answer. He knows and cares, and He brings His ministrations accordingly. Certainly as Gideon later looked back, He must have been extremely thankful for God's gracious patience with him.

B. The Authenticating Sign (6:17-21)

1. *The Meal Prepared (6:17-19)*

Gideon's first response to God's call was to ask for a sign. He wanted to be sure this was God's call. He hadn't yet recognized the Person before him, and he didn't want to be deceived. When the Angel did not respond immediately, Gideon hurried on to ask Him to wait while he prepared food for the two of them to eat. Providing food in this way was a hospitable gesture common to the Middle East. Also, Gideon undoubtedly wanted more time to talk with this welcome Guest. Eating together would provide this. The Angel said He would wait.

As Gideon made preparation, we can see him hurrying from the winepress to his house. There he "made ready a kid, and unleavened cakes of an ephah of flour." This was ample food for two people. A young goat would have provided a large amount of meat, and there was more than a bushel of flour with which to make cakes. Gideon's generosity shows that he was hospitable and that he knew his Visitor was important. Remember that food was extremely scarce after these years of Midianite devastation. After making preparation, Gideon brought out the food and "presented" it to the Angel. Apparently he was satisfied with himself in being willing to supply so liberally of that which was so valuable.

2. *The Sign Provided (6:20, 21)*

It is not clear if Gideon had forgotten about his earlier request for a sign, but the Angel had not. He answered it by directing Gideon in the way to serve the food. This was a little strange—the visitor telling the host how to make the meal ready. Gideon was to spread the meat of the goat and the supply of cakes on the winepress rock. Then he was to pour the valuable, rich "broth" over the meat and cakes that were laid out. This, too, was unusual. Normally food was dipped into broth in order that none would be wasted. Now all would be used quickly, and much would flow off into the ground. Still Gideon carried out orders, recognizing his Visitor's authority. Then the sign was given. The Angel extended the staff, touching the food. Immediately fire consumed it. Gideon then realized what was happening. This was the sign for which he had asked. Then the Angel disappeared.

God gave this sign to encourage Gideon's heart. Gideon would continue to need it as challenging days still lay ahead. Verse 27 indicates that Gideon's brothers and friends misunderstood him; therefore, he would need something sure to which to hold. The sign God gave was one to which Gideon could return day after day to find the renewed courage he needed. Very likely the burned black spot which the fire left on the rock became a hallowed place for him in later days. This was where the Angel had called him. Here he could find the greatest solace and strength for each day's challenge.

C. Gideon's Submission (6:22-24)

We see Gideon's affirmative response to the call by his immediate and complete submission. First, he cried out in fear that he had "seen an angel of the LORD face to face." A clear glimpse of God brings a sense of fear and shame as we see in Job 42:5, 6; Isaiah 6:5 and Luke 5:8. A test of one's spirituality is the degree to which he recognizes his own shortcoming in the presence of the holy God.

A second thing Gideon did was to build an altar, calling it "Jehovah-shalom" (Jehovah is peace). Thus Gideon evidenced his need to worship. A second test of one's spirituality is how much he desires to worship God.

III. The First Assignment (Judg. 6:25-32)

A. Nature and Significance (6:25, 26)

Christians must put away sins in their lives before God can give victory. It was so with Israel. Before they could be delivered from Midian, an altar to Baal must be destroyed. Removing this and cutting down the

Asherah pole nearby was Gideon's first assignment.

The translation "grove" (v. 26) is incorrect. When the King James Version was made, the word was not understood. It refers to a wooden pole, likely lewdly carved, to the goddess Asherah. This pole was to be cut down and used for fuel to fire a new altar which Gideon was to make. He was to sacrifice one of his father's bullocks. This was a dangerous job as the next day's events would indicate. However, it was necessary in order to experience God's blessing.

B. Carrying It Out (6:27)

Gideon did the job in one night with the help of ten servants. He did it at night because there would have been too much opposition in the daytime. The reason for using only his servants was because he could not trust his "household" or "the men of the city."

This was a big job. Baal altars were large. One found at Megiddo in recent years measured some twenty-six feet across and five feet high. It was made of stones and mud fill. It would require time to cut up the pole for fuel with the equipment they had. The bullock had to be brought, killed and prepared for sacrifice; and a new altar had to be built. All eleven men must have worked feverishly to finish the task before morning. As they completed the task, they didn't know what would happen; but they had done God's will despite difficulty and danger. Nothing is as satisfying as doing God's will.

C. Its Shocking Result (6:28-30)

The danger to Gideon was revealed by the people's reaction the next day. They determined to kill the one who had done this thing. They apparently concluded that Gideon had to be the man because only he would have done such a thing. It is not likely that anyone had seen Gideon and his men. If they had, it would have been reported immediately. But Gideon had the reputation of standing for God. This made them think of him. Oh, that Christians today might be known as people of God who dare to stand against Satan's inroads, no matter what the cost may be.

Having reached a conclusion, the townspeople went to the home of Gideon's father, Joash (v. 30). In that day a father had authority over his son. The people wanted Joash to deliver Gideon to them for death because he had committed the deed. How shocking—to want to take the life of a man who had destroyed an altar to Baal and built one to Israel's God!

D. A Remarkable Work of God (6:31, 32)

Before this time Joash may have been weak, permitting the altar to be built on his property (v. 25). But now he became strong. Probably his son's example rebuked him. In effect he said to the people, "Why do you take up Baal's cause in this way? If he is a god, he should be able to take up his own cause. Wait until tomorrow morning and give Baal an opportunity to do this, and let anyone who should attempt to interfere be killed himself." The story implies that his words were accepted and the crowd moved away. Joash's courage and words were important to Gideon and to God's work. All God's people must take their stand for Him so God's work may be accomplished.

Gideon became known as "Jerubbaal," meaning "Baal contender." He was noted for defeating Baal because nothing had happened to him by the morning after he had destroyed Baal's altar. God turned what seemed like sure catastrophe into blessing. Gideon needed this reputation to encourage people to follow him in battle against the Midianites. Had he given the call before gaining the reputation, few would have responded (cf. 6:15). But now he became known all across the country, and people responded. God always works out His plans when one is in His will.

IV. Putting Out the Fleece (Judg. 6:33-40)

A. Gideon's Army (6:33-35)

This reputation apparently came just in time because the enemy soon drew near. God's timetable is always correct! Now when Gideon called for people to come to fight the Midianites, they responded in surprising number. They came from Gideon's home area, Abiezer; from his home tribe, Manasseh, and then from Asher, Zebulun and Naphtali. All were near at hand. Gideon was filled by "the Spirit of the LORD" at this time. Being filled by God's Spirit is the secret of success for God in any day. After God gave Gideon the reputation, He empowered him with the Holy Spirit.

B. Gideon's Fear (6:36)

Here Gideon displayed weakness. He became fearful and sought reassurance from God. This fear was prompted by his comparatively small number of inept soldiers. The response was surprisingly good, and Gideon must have rejoiced at first. But when he saw the huge number of the enemy, his group seemed small. The enemy numbered no less than 135,000 (Judg. 8:10); Gideon's group, only 32,000 (Judg. 7:3). This was a large disparity, but still Gideon should have trusted. However, he reacted as many Christians do today.

C. The Sign of the Fleece (6:37-40)

As a result, Gideon thought of a test by which God could indicate His will. He laid a fleece of wool out on the ground overnight. He asked that if he were to proceed, it would be wet in the morning while the ground remained dry. The next morning the fleece was wet. Then he asked God to keep it dry the next night while making the ground wet. Again God complied. Then Gideon led the army against the enemy.

D. The Grace of God

Was Gideon right in asking God for this sign? The answer is "no." Two main reasons support this. First, God had already told Gideon what He wanted (6:14-16). There was no reason for further confirmation. In putting forth the test, Gideon was not asking what God wanted but whether or not God would be pleased to change what He had earlier ordered. When God makes an assignment, that is what He wants done, no matter the difficulty or time.

The other reason is that Gideon devised the type of test, saying that God had to do it or else he, Gideon, would not obey. When God did as Gideon asked the first time, Gideon insisted that He do it a second time, only in a reverse manner. He broke his word to God on this count, and this compounded the error. Christians are not to lay down conditions to God. God had already provided the proper kind of sign. That was the remarkable gathering of 32,000 followers to Gideon when only shortly before there would probably have been none at all. Gideon had witnessed this quick and amazing change and should have been reassured by this—if he needed reassurance—without having to resort to this improper trick.

Sometimes it is said that God would not have responded to Gideon by making the fleece wet and then dry if what Gideon did was wrong. However, God often blesses in spite of what Christians do, not because of it. This was the case here. God was gracious toward His servant, ministering to him patiently, knowing the heavy burden that Gideon had been bearing and the great challenge facing him.

Prepare To Answer Intelligently

1. What did the "prophet" say to the Israelites?
2. How did the Angel show tenderness toward Gideon in giving the call?
3. When did Gideon realize Who his Visitor was?
4. In what ways was the sign, which the Angel chose to give Gideon, especially helpful to him?
5. Why was it necessary that the Baal altar be destroyed?
6. How did the townspeople react to its destruction?
7. How did Gideon's new reputation help to prepare for the coming battle with the Midianites?
8. How many men responded to his call to battle?
9. Why did Gideon suddenly become fearful?
10. What was the main reason Gideon was wrong in asking the sign he did?

CHAPTER 6

The Defeat of the Midianites

BIBLE PORTION TO READ: Judges 7:1-25

NOW WE SHALL CONSIDER one of the best known battles of the Bible, that of Gideon's three hundred against the Midianites. This shows what even a few can do when God is on their side.

I. The Army Reduced in Size (Judg. 7:1-6)

The chapter first concerns God's manner of adjusting the size of Gideon's army. The direction of the adjustment astonished and surprised Gideon. Gideon had thought an adjustment was needed, true enough; but he thought the army should be increased in size so that it would match the Midianite throng of 135,000. However, God decreased the size of the army. Gideon's army of 32,000, although already less than a fourth the number of the enemy, was too large. It must be made smaller.

Here we have an illustration of Romans 8:26. Gideon thought that he needed more soldiers, but God knew he needed fewer. When God's people of any day judge according to their own sense of values and needs, they often see these needs to be different from the way God sees them. Therefore, their prayers are improper. The Holy Spirit must make "intercession" for them to another end so they will receive God's best.

A. The Setting (7:1)

In verse 1 we see the setting of this event. It was at the "well of Harod" opposite the "hill of Moreh." The "well of Harod" is at the foot of Mount Gilboa at the southern edge of the Esdraelon valley. The "hill of Moreh" is in the middle of the valley, to the north. Thus the Midianites were quartered in the valley between these two points with Gideon's army on the mountain side to the south. Both names of Gideon—Jerubbaal and Gideon—were used here as he assembled his troops in this place. This is significant in that his troops thought of him in the sense of both names. Not only was he Gideon; but he was Jerubbaal, the one who had defeated Baal (cf. lesson 5, Judg. 6:32).

B. The Reason for the Reduction (7:2)

Next we see why Gideon's forces were reduced. God saw that this reduction was necessary in order that Gideon's army would be willing to give God the credit for the victory when it happened, rather than taking the credit themselves. Gideon's army was already less than a fourth the size of the enemy's, but God knew this disparity was not enough to bring the people to recognize God's divine hand in the resulting victory. They would still say they had done it, probably boasting even more since the odds against them were so great.

Note two important thoughts. First, men are very self-centered and tend to take credit for things accomplished even when that credit is not due them. This is true in man's interrelation with other men. When something good is brought about, each one involved tends to think of himself as being mainly responsible. To him, his importance and contribution appear to be greater than that of others. This leads to pride on his part and also to hurt feelings if others do not applaud him accordingly. This is even more true in man's relationship to God. The Christian easily takes all credit to himself. He feels the good work done has been because of his efforts. He forgets that God has used him only as an instrument and that God is the One Who has planned and effected the work. Every Christian should constantly remind himself of his own inadequacy and full dependence on God and that God is the One to receive the honor and glory.

The second thought is that man's own plans and program may actually hinder God's work rather than help it. Gideon had 32,000 in his army. As he returned to them after God had graciously reassured him by the use of the fleece, he no doubt planned how he would use them to bring about the victory. True, the army was small; but by manipulating them, he would defeat the enemy. We may be sure that he was glad the number was no less than it was; since it was this large, he would be able to accomplish the goal since God had promised him he would. Actually, however, Gideon's plans and this number of 32,000 stood in the way of God's giving the victory. Because of the people's hearts, God could not use these 32,000. Neither the number nor Gideon's plans were wrong in themselves. God could have used them if they had been in His will. What was wrong was that, being what they were, God would not receive the glory for the victory. Therefore, the number and plans stood in the way.

There is nothing wrong in making plans to do God's work today, providing the planning is kept in the right perspective. Christians must realize that all plans are to be directed by the Lord and that the Lord is to receive *all* glory in the end—not the human instruments who make the plans. God can use good planning and numbers of people to effect them. Indeed, good plans should be made. But when they are, it must first be recognized that they are ordered by the Lord Himself; and second, they must be kept subservient in importance to God's blessing. Then, when the work has been completed, all glory is to be rendered to God for it, recognizing that both plans and numbers of people involved were only God's instruments to do the work.

C. The First Reduction (7:3)

After telling why the number must be reduced, God showed Gideon how this should be done. He was to announce to his troops that everyone who was "fearful and afraid" should "return and depart early from mount Gilead." That is, everyone who feared the enemy and was therefore not a good soldier anyway should go home. This made good sense as all God's directions do. Those who feared the enemy so much that they were willing to admit it were not good members of Gideon's army. They would not serve well in combat, and they would also hurt the morale of others. Probably it had been the presence of these, as well as the great disparity of numbers with the Midianites, that caused Gideon's heart to faint earlier. Not only was his army small, but it was not of good quality. Now God was about to change this situation.

At the time Gideon had no way of knowing just how much of a reduction in numbers God had in mind. Earlier Gideon had thought the army was too small, not too large; and it would have been a major adjustment of mind for him to think of any reduction at all. Very likely, then, he was thinking only of a small reduction —maybe two or three hundred at the most. Therefore, when God said that all the fearful should return home, he must have thought quickly of how many this would entail. Wishful thinking would have made him think that these would be few in number. What consternation and chagrin must have been his when he saw no less than 22,000 stand up and leave. Can't you imagine him giving the message allowing them to leave in a way that would not encourage any more than necessary to go? Thus, when two out of every three suddenly arose to depart, he probably began to protest. Did the men really understand him? They didn't *have* to go. But when they were permitted to leave, two out of three moved away; then Gideon was left with what must have seemed like an impossibly small handful— only 10,000. Whereas the odds before had been four to one, now they had become more than thirteen to one. How could so many Midianites ever be defeated by so few Israelites?

Although nothing is said regarding weapons, it is certain that a major disparity existed with the enemy in regard to equipment. Since the Midianites had come to fight, they would have been well armed. On the other hand, since the Israelites had been victims of oppression during the past six years, they would have had few weapons. The Midianites would have confiscated all they found, along with the grain and livestock. In fact, evidence that this was true is seen from the weapons Gideon's troops finally used: trumpets, pitchers and lamps! These were not conventional arms. Not only was Gideon left with a very small army but one that was poorly equipped. Indeed he must have wondered at God's wisdom in all this.

God will often let His children face situations like this today in order to test them. What kind of Christians are they? What sort of faith do they possess? Do they really believe God can do the impossible? Are they ready to trust Him when all seems hopeless and black? God is more interested in the quality of His people than in their victories. He wants Christians to grow, to mature and to learn to trust Him fully. He also has the necessary victories in mind, and He will take care of those; but He wants the development and the growth of His children even more. Tests are allowed to come accordingly.

D. The Second Reduction (7:4-6)

The first troop reduction was difficult for Gideon to accept; but how astonished he must have been when God said, "The people are yet too many." Gideon believed his troops were far too few now; but God was saying that this was not so. Of course, God was placing his evaluation on the basis of the need for reduction given to Gideon in the first place. The people, even at odds of thirteen to one, would not give God the honor when the victory had been won. Therefore, the number had to be reduced still more. This is a significant commentary on how self-centered God's people are. They take all credit to themselves if there is any way to do so.

This time God reduced the army by a test at the water's edge. The water was likely that from the "well of Harod," which still exists. Today the state of Israel has made a beautiful park of the area with an attractive pool formed by the water from this spring. Gideon was to bring his 10,000 remaining troops to the water to drink. Those who drank by bringing water to their mouths with their hands (v. 6) were to be kept as soldiers, but those who bowed "down upon his [their] knees to drink" were to be sent home. Verse 5 is a bit confusing when it speaks of the first group as lapping the water "as a dog lappeth." The thought is probably of lapping the water in this manner out of one's hand after bringing it to the mouth. The contrast, clearly, is between those who bowed down fully to drink directly from the stream and those who put their hands down to bring the water to the mouth. The first group showed themselves more interested in satisfying personal needs; the latter indicated that they were interested in remaining vigilant to meet the enemy should he come on them as they knelt to drink.

Today many of God's children are more interested in their personal needs than in God's work. Their interest is their own satisfaction, not the church or the need for reaching the lost for Christ. However, God wants those in His army who put His work first and let their own interests take second place.

Only three hundred were properly qualified to be soldiers. This means that 9,700 bowed down to drink, demonstrating themselves to be unsuitable to serve. How dismayed Gideon must have been. How could God save Israel with this tiny handful?

Notice that fewer than 1 percent were good soldiers. What would be the percentage of true soldiers in an average fundamental church today? The question should make us think.

II. Further Reassurance (Judg. 7:7-15)

A. By God's Direct Word (7:7)

God reassured Gideon in two ways. He understood His servant's astonishment and need of encouragement. He demonstrated His grace in the way He filled that need. First He stated, "By the three hundred men that lapped will I save you." In other words God was saying, "Yes, Gideon, though you cannot see how, still in truth, by such a small number as this 300 who showed themselves real soldiers by the way they chose to drink, Israel will be saved. You can be sure of this because I the Lord will do it." When Christians have God on their side, no matter how small the number, the victory is sure. One Christian *with* God is a majority.

B. By the Midianite's Dream (7:8-15)

Gideon carried out God's directives in sending the 9,700 home. Then God encouraged him in a second way. He told Gideon to go by night (taking Phurah, his servant, along if he was afraid to go alone) to the Midianite camp and listen to what the enemy was saying. Gideon obeyed. He found that the enemy was "like grasshoppers for multitude" (v. 12). He overheard one Midianite tell another of a dream he had in which a "cake of barley bread" had tumbled into the camp and struck a tent, making it fall. The companion said this signified Gideon's coming against the Midianite camp, overthrowing it. Barley bread was the bread of the poor. Here it symbolized Gideon as Israel's leader; it was appropriate symbolism because the Midianites considered Israel to be a weak, poor people. Making a tent to fall was significant because to the Midianites, who were desert dwellers, one's tent was all-important as one's home. The falling of the tent here meant that the whole camp would be destroyed. Apparently the Midianites had learned that a man named Gideon was assembling an army against them, and this Midianite recognized a sign that he would succeed.

When Gideon overheard this conversation, he was encouraged as God had said he would be. He first "worshipped" God for encouraging him; then he returned to rally his men for the attack. God knows how to encourage His soldiers in their battle for Him. It may come in unlikely ways. The Christian should recognize it quickly, then praise God even as Gideon did.

III. The Great Victory (Judg. 7:16-25)

A. The Plan (7:16-18)

On returning to his troops, Gideon outlined the plan of attack God had revealed to him. The three hundred were to be divided into three companies, presumably of equal size, with each man armed with a trumpet, an empty pitcher and a lamp (or torch) inside the pitcher. The companies were to move against the enemy at night, coming from three different directions at the same time. When Gideon would blow his trumpet, they were to blow theirs and cry, "The sword of the LORD, and of Gideon."

B. The Attack (7:19, 20)

With the plan thus outlined, Gideon, with his one hundred, moved down into position; and the other two companies apparently spread along the mountainside to show an extended front. This was just after the setting of the "middle watch" of the night, the midnight hour. When all was ready, Gideon signaled. All three companies blew their trumpets and broke their pitchers. The breaking pitchers exposed the lighted lamps (or torches) inside, thus making a sudden great noise from the breaking of the pottery and a sudden blaze of light from the three hundred lamps. With this noise and light coming from three different areas on the mountain at the same time, the enemy believed an immense host was charging down on them. All three hundred also shouted their ringing battle cry, "The sword of the LORD, and of Gideon."

C. The Victory (7:21, 22)

Verse 21 appears to mean that Gideon's men remained at a distance. This kept them from being hurt in the melee that immediately broke out. The host of the Midianites "ran, and cried, and fled." They started to run to get away from the imagined great host. First they would have started to run north to get away from the charging "throng" coming down the mountain on the south; then they would have veered east to move toward the Jordan in the direction of home.

The first part of verse 22 seems to summarize the happening briefly. As a result of the sudden sound and light, the enemy's first reaction was to take a sword against his own friend. In the darkness, they couldn't tell friends from foe; and—in the terror of the imagined attack—they struck any moving person as an enemy. Thus many Midianites were killed quickly, even though Gideon's men had not entered the camp. Likely after the first outbreak of fighting, the actual flight got underway. The last half of verse 22 tells which direction they went. It was toward the Jordan where the city of Abel-meholah was. Abel-meholah later became Elisha's hometown (1 Kings 19:16).

This was a remarkable victory. As Gideon saw the enemy's flight, represented by their quickly moving lights, he must have raised a prayer of thanksgiving to God. God had said this would happen, and it had. How thrilled Gideon must have been and how his faith must have been encouraged.

God's way is always best. Often it is difficult to see the wisdom in God's way, but the wisdom is there. Then, after the wisdom has been demonstrated, there is the thrill of recognizing the plan and thanking God for it.

D. The Fruitful Result (7:23-25)

Gideon's first move, after this initial aspect of victory, was to send for men (probably for those of the 32,000 who had recently left him) out of Naphtali, Asher and

Manasseh and have them come to help pursue the fleeing enemy.

Then Gideon sent the Ephraimites to the south to ask that they quickly seize "the waters unto Bethbarah and Jordan" to intercept the fleeing Midianites. These were likely the "waters" which the enemy would have to cross. This required time, but the Ephraimites accomplished much of what Gideon wanted. The Midianites had flocks and herds to take along; so they moved slowly. After the first rush to flee, they likely paused to regroup. Most of their weapons and provisions would have been left in the camp; therefore, any return was out of the question. Thus the Ephraimites were able to take many of the crucial fording places in time to stop them. Among those killed were two Midianite leaders.

With this help from the Ephraimites, along with the return of men from the other three tribes, Gideon must have been encouraged. God was good, providing and supplying in these additional ways. In the strength thus received, Gideon pursued the enemy.

Prepare To Answer Intelligently

1. Why did God deem it necessary that Gideon's 32,000 be reduced?
2. How was the first reduction to be made?
3. What was the test for the second reduction?
4. What percentage of Gideon's original army finally proved to be good soldiers?
5. What was the dream that Gideon heard in the camp of the Midianites?
6. Why did God want Gideon to hear it?
7. What were the weapons used by Gideon's army?
8. How did they prove to be effective weapons?
9. What effect did their use have on the Midianites?
10. What were the Ephraimites asked to do?

CHAPTER 7

Aftermath of Victory

BIBLE PORTION TO READ: Judges 8:1-35

IT IS ONE THING to win victories; it is another to follow through after victories so that a full benefit is obtained. Gideon had won a splendid victory over the Midianites, but a different pursuit was needed as a follow-through. Let us consider the pursuit and some unusual events connected with it, as well as some truths that will be of profit today.

I. The Jealousy of Ephraim (Judg. 8:1-3)

Jealousy has always existed among God's people. It seriously hinders God's work, bringing divisions and hard feelings. More than once Ephraim displayed a jealous feeling toward the other tribes, and one of those times occurred here with Gideon (cf. also Judg. 12:1-6).

A. Ephraim's Unjust Complaint (8:1)

Ephraim's jealous complaint was very strange. They had done well to hinder the fleeing Midianites and kill two of their leaders at the Jordan crossing, but they complained that Gideon hadn't called them to aid against this enemy in the first place. Gideon had asked help from Manasseh, Asher, Zebulun and Naphtali (Judg. 6:35); but he hadn't turned to Ephraim. This was understandable, for Ephraim lived too far south to be involved in the Midianite raids. However, Ephraim was a proud tribe, and her people wanted to be the leaders in all tribal matters. The text says that they complained "sharply"; they were serious and ready to make a problem for Gideon. Thus they tried to keep him from pursuing the Midianites at a time when every minute counted.

Jealousy has no place in God's work. Any time it appears, it works to an evil end, causing strife and contention. Those involved strive with each other rather than pursuing Satan's forces. Often, too, those who are jealous press their complaints severely—as did the Ephraimites—so that weeks and even months are involved in heated controversy. Jealousy arises because of proud hearts. People feel that they have been slighted when they deserve better. We need to heed the Lord Jesus' words in Matthew 20:26 and 27. If followed, they would alleviate and solve many problems.

B. Gideon's Careful Answer (8:2, 3)

We must give Gideon high credit for answering as he did. He might have responded heatedly, for Ephraim was certainly in the wrong. But if he had, there would have been greater difficulty and probably no Midianites would have been pursued. Instead, Gideon sought an answer that would assuage the hurt feelings and avoid the problem. He complimented them on what they had done, in effect letting them think that they had done more than he had. They, rather than he, had killed Oreb and Zeeb, the two Midianite leaders. What they had done was like harvesting Ephraim's grapes (which they thought were the finest) in comparison with the vintage of the grapes of Abi-ezer (family name of Gideon's ancestry). This must have been difficult for Gideon to say when the Ephraimites were wrong and Gideon was the one mainly responsible—under God— for the whole victory. However, the implied compliment worked, and Gideon was able to undertake the task at hand.

The Christian, especially a pastor, who is willing and able to reply kindly and carefully in times of crisis is a wise person. What one says at such a time can easily make the difference between a prolonged quarrel or a passing incident. It takes strong self-control, as well as good common sense and intelligence, to do so; but the result makes any demand more than worthwhile.

II. Pursuit of the Midianites (Judg. 8:4-10)

With this explosive crisis alleviated, Gideon could proceed with the important business at hand. He could pursue the Midianites and defeat them completely, thus keeping them from returning against Israel.

A. The Pursuit Proper (8:4, 10)

Verse 4 speaks only of the same three hundred men who continued with Gideon. The implication is that those from Manasseh, Naphtali and Asher who had returned to help in the pursuit (Judg. 7:23) stayed only long enough to insure that the enemy was put to rout while still west of Jordan. When this had been accomplished, they apparently returned home for the second time. With the faithful three hundred, Gideon took up the chase, crossing to the east side of Jordan. It seems that the Midianites, who had not been killed, were able to move quickly enough to stay ahead of Gideon; for, according to verse 10, Gideon didn't encounter them until he reached their land. The Karkor (v. 10) is still unidentified but was probably near modern Ammon, the ancient capital of the Ammonites and present capital of Jordan.

B. Uncooperative Israelites (8:5-9)

Not only did Gideon have to deal with the jealous Ephraimites; but when he had crossed the Jordan, he met fearful, uncooperative Israelites there. He needed provisions for his three hundred. He drew near to the city of Succoth and asked the people for "loaves of bread" to sustain his men as they pursued "after Zebah and Zalmunna." Undoubtedly he expected an agreeable response since these, too, were Israelites, and the Midianites were their enemy. Therefore, the answer in verse 6 must have been extremely disappointing. The inhabitants of Succoth weren't about to jeopardize their safety by helping Gideon's men because the Ammonites might retaliate. True, Gideon had just delivered their fellow tribesmen on the other side of Jordan from this enemy, but they wouldn't help him if doing so might cause them hurt in days to come. Gideon, then, must provide for his own army. The inhabitants of Succoth wouldn't get involved.

Gideon was shocked and angered. He warned them that, in view of such lack of cooperation, he himself would bring retaliation against them after God had delivered Zebah and Zalmunna into his hand. Then he moved on to the next Israelite city, Penuel, making the same request. Here Gideon met with the same lack of cooperation, for these people also feared the Midianites. Gideon warned them what he would do when he returned, saying that he would "break down this tower," evidently referring to a prominent tower in the city. We do not know where Gideon found the necessary food, but he did so and continued to move on against the enemy.

Here is an illustration of a sad truth regarding too many present-day Christians. Great numbers of God's people do not want to become involved in God's work. They do not want to declare themselves as on God's or Satan's side. It might hurt their business. They might not be well accepted socially or could suffer loss in position if they should make too much of their Christianity or become known as "fanatics" in religious matters. They let someone else do the work of the church or else let the work suffer. In due time these people will experience loss at God's hand for this attitude. They may think they will avoid loss at the world's hand, but they won't at God's hand. The people of Succoth and Penuel were cowards, unwilling to stand for what they knew was right.

III. Defeat of the Midianites (Judg. 8:11-13, 18-21)
A. The Defeat Proper (8:11-13)

Gideon still had to encounter an army of 15,000

(v. 10), a sizable group for 300 to attack! Some 120,000 had been killed either in the first encounter or at the crossing of the Jordan when confronted by the Ephraimites. Gideon found this number quartered near two centers, called Nobah and Jogbehah. The phrase "for the host was secure" means that Gideon took the enemy by surprise. They thought they were secure from such an attack. They had been able to get all the way home and probably thought that those pursuing would have given up long ago. However, they did not know Gideon's tenacity. As a result, he was able to make a surprise attack which, no doubt, contributed significantly to the success experienced. Once more the enemy fled with Gideon pursuing. The two main leaders, Zebah and Zalmunna, were captured.

Gideon must be commended. He pursued the enemy for many miles, procuring provisions for his troops as he could. He had encountered the Ephraimites' jealousy and the noncooperation of fellow Israelites. It would have been easier not to have started, much less to continue in the face of these problems. But Gideon had persisted. The Midianites must be defeated thoroughly. Thus these leaders had to be removed so they would not turn on the Israelites again.

Gideon thus demonstrated the faithfulness and courage which all of God's servants need in their battle for God. Often one finds it easy to quit entirely, but God desires His warriors to press on.

B. The Slaying of Zebah and Zalmunna (8:18-21)

At first Gideon didn't take the two leaders' lives but kept them alive to show the people of Succoth and Penuel that he had captured them (cf. vv. 15-17).

However, this done, he turned to the matter of punishing the two. Gideon had learned they were responsible for the death of a group of Israelites at Tabor. Thus he asked them, "What manner of men were they whom ye slew at Tabor?" They replied, "As thou art, so were they; each one resembled the children of a king." Thus Gideon knew that these had been his own two brothers. This decided the issue of the two kings. Probably Gideon had surmised who comprised this group. This may have been one reason for his pressing on to capture these men. He determined to have their lives. First he directed his firstborn son, Jether, to do the job; but Jether was fearful, being yet young. Then Gideon himself killed the two. Thus he was avenged of the blood of his brothers, and Israel no longer had to fear the Midianites.

IV. Punishment of Succoth and Penuel (Judg. 8:14-17)

A. The Punishment Itself

Gideon was a man of his word. When Succoth and Penuel had refused to aid Gideon's troops in pursuing the enemy, he had warned them that he would return after he accomplished his mission. After they had refused to assist him, Gideon had additional reason to capture the two Midianite leaders. Succoth's and Penuel's refusal indicated they didn't think he could capture these men. Therefore, he first met this challenge, then returned to punish the two cities.

Gideon first approached Succoth. Before entering the city, he captured a young man of the city and learned the names of the city's leaders. The Hebrew says that the boy "wrote down" their names. Thus Gideon knew the leaders responsible for refusing his request. He entered the city and showed the people his two prizes, the two Midianite leaders, letting all know that he had accomplished what they had doubted he could. Then he took "thorns of the wilderness and briers" and "taught the men of Succoth." He used these thorns and briers on each of the seventy-seven leaders. The thorns and briers would have torn their flesh (v. 7). Gideon didn't take their lives then, but he caused them to suffer pain.

When this had been done to the men of Succoth, Gideon went to Penuel where the leaders had also refused him. He had forewarned them that their "tower" would be destroyed. He now did this and also killed "the men of the city." We don't know why he went this far.

B. A Valuable Lesson

These Israelites who wouldn't get involved in defeating the enemy of God's people were now punished for their wrong decisions. They had thought they were "playing it safe" by not helping Gideon, but they were wrong. God punishes, sometimes severely.

Christians who dabble in sin and refuse to be truly on the Lord's side in the battle with Satan often think they are "playing it safe." But they only fool themselves. God will bring His reprimand.

V. A Good and Bad Action (Judg. 8:22-27)

A. The Good Action (8:22, 23)

When Gideon returned home after this successful campaign, many people wanted to proclaim him king, as hereditary ruler. No other judge had received this offer. They had simply continued in the capacity of judges, having no official title and with no thought of their position being passed on to descendants. Gideon refused the offer made to him (Judg. 8:23). Gideon recognized the theocratic form of government God had instituted, and he wisely refused the honor extended to him.

Gideon was right in this action. A lesser person probably would have accepted the offer with pride. Pride is one of Satan's most insidious weapons to defeat Christians.

B. The Bad Action (8:24-27)

Gideon replied well in this respect, but then he said something wrong. He asked the people to bring him the "earrings" that had been taken as spoil from the defeated Midianites so he could make an "ephod." This was an article of clothing prescribed by God for the high priest. It was a sort of extravagant apron (Exod. 28:6), covering the front and back of the person. On the front was the linen "breastplate" in which the Urim and Thummim were kept.

It is easy to see the reason for Gideon's request. He had heard remarkable revelation from God, something normally reserved for the high priest. Though he turned down the kingship, he wanted this "priestly" function to continue. He may have argued that the true high priest of the day was not doing his job (which certainly was true); therefore, someone needed to do it better. If he, Gideon, were to serve in this way, he needed an ephod which went with the office.

The people responded to Gideon's request. They brought the earrings, and the weight was 1700 shekels (about 42 pounds). This was more than Gideon needed. They also brought other materials to make the ephod. Gideon made it and placed it in his hometown, Ophrah. Then "all Israel went thither a whoring after it." The people sinned by coming to Gideon instead of the regular high priest to hear God's revelations. They believed he received these revelations because he had this ephod. Thus Gideon usurped the high priest's rightful position, and the people sinned in giving Gideon this recognition.

However good Gideon's motivation may have been, and no matter how poorly the true high priest of the day was doing his work, God's prescribed law was not that a person like Gideon, who was not even a Levite, should take the high priest's position. Therefore, Gideon and the people were wrong in their actions.

God has prescribed methods in His Word for doing His work. These are to be observed in any day.

VI. Final Notes Regarding Gideon (Judg. 8:28-35)
A. Peace in Israel (8:28, 29)

The chapter closes with a few miscellaneous notes, mainly directed as background for the tragic episode related in the next chapter. Verse 28 says that Midian remained subdued following Gideon's day. Thus the land had peace over forty years. Gideon continued to live in his own home during this time (v. 29).

B. Gideon's Family and Death (8:30-32)

Verses 30-32 give more particular information as background for chapter 9. Gideon had forty sons (v. 30) who were later killed by Abimelech (9:5). The birth of Abimelech, the renegade son, is recorded in verse 31. His mother was a concubine of Gideon. This means that Gideon's sin with this woman resulted in this birth. Sin regularly leads to sorrow.

Verse 32 tells of Gideon's death, being buried in Ophrah, the hometown. Gideon's death made possible the event concerning the renegade son, Abimelech.

C. Israelite Apostasy Again (8:33-35)

After Gideon's death, the people reverted to Baal worship. They forgot it was God Who delivered them. They also forgot to be kind to Gideon's house after the one to whom they were indebted died.

All this shows how fickle God's people are. They may follow God's way for a time if they have a strong leader, but they easily change to their own way if that leader dies or conditions change.

God delights in His children's doing His will faithfully, no matter the leadership or the conditions.

Prepare To Answer Intelligently

1. Of what did Ephraim complain to Gideon?
2. What was admirable in Gideon's response to the Ephraimites?
3. Why does jealousy often harm God's work?
4. Why did Succoth and Penuel refuse to help Gideon's army?
5. What was Gideon offered when he returned home?
6. Why would Gideon have been wrong in accepting?
7. What request did Gideon then make of the people?
8. What sin was involved in this request?
9. What great sin did the people commit after Gideon died?

CHAPTER 8

Abimelech, the Renegade King

BIBLE PORTION TO READ: Judges 9:1-57

THIS CHAPTER concerns a tragic interlude in the Period of the Judges. Abimelech, one of Gideon's sons, had himself crowned king in direct opposition to the theocratic order established by God. Abimelech used unscrupulous methods to do so, lived a stormy three years in keeping with his position and died as a result of a millstone thrown on his head.

I. Establishment As King (Judg. 9:1-6)

The name "Abimelech" means "king's father." What prompted Gideon to give this name to his son is not indicated, but the son did show an unusual desire for kingship when he came of age. Since his mother lived in Shechem, he approached his relatives there to ask that they proclaim him king. He argued that it would be better for them to be ruled by a person related to them than by Gideon's other sons who were not. Apparently Abimelech believed that the other sons also shared his desire to rule, although there is no evidence that they did. He must have been a persuasive person, for his relatives acceded. They, in turn, persuaded other Shechemites who gave Abimelech seventy pieces of silver with which to press his campaign.

Abimelech used this money to hire "vain and light" helpers. With these he went to Ophrah, Gideon's hometown, and killed his seventy half brothers, with the exception of the younger, Jotham, who hid himself. Having killed those, he returned to Shechem where he was proclaimed king. Perhaps he didn't tell them what he had just done at Ophrah.

The territory Abimelech ruled at one time is not given, but probably it wasn't extensive. Most of the action in the story took place around Shechem, and it may be that only people within a few miles radius recognized the renegade king. His rule lasted only three years. Despite its brevity, its story was included in the sacred record because it was one more sinful deviation occurring in the Period of the Judges and also because its result significantly illustrates the way God effects the divine principle of Galatians 6:7.

II. Opposition of Jotham (Judg. 9:7-21)

A. The Person (9:7, 21)

Jotham, Gideon's youngest son, had courage and ability. Having learned of Abimelech's coronation, he came to Mount Gerizim, beside Shechem. There he proclaimed a parable for the Shechemites to hear. The parable illustrated the Shechemites' folly in crowning Abimelech king. Having given it, he moved away quickly.

It is important to speak against sin, even though one must stand alone. Many Christians think there is little use in trying when people generally don't seem to care. But God looks for those who are concerned enough to do what they can, no matter how little.

B. The Parable (9:8-20)

1. *The Parable Itself (9:8-15)*

The parable concerned the selection of a tree to reign as king over other trees. First the kingship was offered to the olive tree, then to the fig tree and then to the grapevine. Each refused the honor because of its important task. At last the kingship was offered to the lowly, worthless bramble. It readily accepted (9:15).

2. *The Significance (9:16-20)*

The point of the parable was that the Shechemites, in crowning Abimelech king, had chosen one who was like the worthless bramble when compared with the olive and fig trees and grapevine. Olives, figs and grapes were highly valued crops, while the bramble brier was good only to burn. By this parable Jotham reminded his hearers to remember that Gideon had turned down the kingship; and he implied that the other sons, now slain, would have done likewise. The Shechemites had anointed the least capable member of Gideon's family. Jotham reminded them of Gideon's high character in speaking of the deliverance he had effected over the Midianites (v. 17), and he told them of the massacre of his sons in case they hadn't been told (v. 18). His closing words were that the Shechemites had displayed extreme ingratitude toward Gideon in spite of all that Gideon had done for them; then he pronounced what amounted to a curse on both the Shechemites and Abimelech.

The words of the bramble were noteworthy: "Put your trust in my shadow." The bramble had no shadow, and the Shechemites would learn shortly that Abimelech had nothing in which they could trust.

Choice of leadership is always important. Sometimes little thought is given to the selection of people for church offices. Thus people with limited qualifications are often given responsibility and with unhappy consequences. Much prayer and careful thought should characterize every church election. Too, only offices approved by God are to be created and filled. God did not want His people to have a king then.

III. Opposition of Shechemites (Judg. 9:22-29)

A. By the Shechemites Alone (9:22-25)

Jotham's parable bore little fruit for three years, but finally the Shechemites realized the mistake they had made. Dissension arose between ruler and people. Jotham's parable had probably first stimulated the people to think; then God used Abimelech's continuing improper tactics to convince them. Thus the people began to work against Abimelech by placing "liers in wait for him in the top of the mountains" (Gerizim and Ebal, one on each side of Shechem). These "liers in wait" robbed caravan travelers, thus bringing discredit on Abimelech's rule. Also they sought to kill Abimelech himself. However, Abimelech learned of the activity and sought a way of reprisal.

Apparently God brought about this dissension. Sometimes it seems that unjust rulers continue in power without opposition and that God doesn't care that innocent people suffer. However, God knows and cares about such occasions and will do what is best in the time and way He sees best. The Christian must rest in God's wisdom and power (Rom. 12:19).

B. With Gaal's Help (9:26-29)

As strife developed, the Shechemites received unexpected help. A man named Gaal, a sort of knight-errant of the day, came to them. He seems to have been moving through the country with a group of "brethren" (likely fellow fighters) to engage in quarrels of this kind, no doubt for material gain. The Shechemites put "their confidence in him."

Sometime after he arrived, a day of feasting was held in "the house of their god." At the feast Gaal made a speech, challenging Abimelech. He urged that he, Gaal, be made head over the Shechemites. It seems that he was asking to be given this position in place of Zebul, whom Abimelech had installed. The story makes clear that Zebul was working in Abimelech's behalf against the Shechemites in the strife that had developed, and apparently Gaal had learned of this. The Shechemites seem to have acceded to Gaal's request.

Abimelech wasn't living in Shechem then. He likely sought to widen his scope of rule by moving about. Thus he learned of developments from other sources.

It is not easy to know how to assess Gaal. He appeared at an opportune time for the people of Shechem, and he provided needed leadership. Certainly the Shechemites believed that he would benefit them. However, in an ensuing battle he was badly beaten and driven out of Shechem. Was he God's provision at the time, or did the Shechemites do wrong in trusting him? One thing should be noted: Any person or group should use care in respect to those they choose as leaders. Someone whose background is unknown is seldom the best one to select. He may be an opportunist. One must exercise great care in choosing a leader.

IV. Battle with Abimelech (Judg. 9:30-41)

A. Zebul the Informer (9:30-34)

Although Zebul was Abimelech's friend, he stayed in the city and wasn't treated as an enemy by the Shechemites. Perhaps the people didn't believe he was on Abimelech's side. He learned of Gaal's challenge, noting how the people accepted Gaal. He sent messengers to Abimelech with the news. He told him about Gaal and how to proceed. Abimelech should come to Shechem by night and lie in wait with his men on the mountainside. Then in the early morning, he should attack as Gaal and the Shechemites moved out of the city. Abimelech followed the advice, dividing his men into four groups to lie in wait.

B. Gaal and Zebul (9:35-38)

In the morning, after Abimelech had arrived in the fields, Gaal appeared at the city gate. Perhaps he had begun a regular early morning reconnaissance to see if there were signs of Abimelech's presence. This morning he saw Abimelech's men moving. When Gaal pointed out the movement to Zebul who was there, Zebul said that Gaal was mistaken in thinking these were men moving; they were only shadows on the mountainside. But as Gaal kept watching, he saw two groups of men moving and stated so. Zebul saw there was no longer use of pretending, so he challenged him to move out and fight, admitting that these were Abimelech's men.

One result of this interchange was that Zebul held Gaal back for a time from attacking, giving Abimelech an advantage. Also Zebul's loyalties were revealed. Gaal moved quickly to counter Abimelech's attack.

C. The Defeat of Gaal (9:39-41)

The battle now joined. It seems that Gaal led his men quickly out of the city to meet Abimelech's forces. He led "men of Shechem." These were likely his own followers and men of Shechem in general.

Abimelech's troops proved to be superior in the struggle. Gaal's men were defeated, being driven back inside the city. However, Abimelech didn't force his way into the city at this moment. He withdrew to Arumah, a place probably near Shechem.

Inside the city, Zebul discredited Gaal before the citizens, then forced him to leave. Probably the two men had vied with each other for the Shechemites' trust during the prior days. As long as Gaal appeared to have the upper hand, the people had followed him; but with this defeat they reverted to Zebul. Gaal probably accused Zebul of being a traitor, telling the people of his words at the gate that morning. Zebul must have denied the accusations, winning the people's favor. Thus Gaal had to leave, and Zebul again controlled the city. This pleased Abimelech.

In times of such contention, people have to discern between truth and falsehood. Actually Gaal was much more right than Zebul. Whatever kind of person he was, Gaal certainly tried to do the best for Shechem; but Zebul worked for Abimelech. Yet, because Gaal couldn't win this battle, the people turned against him and believed Zebul's lie. This often happens. People need to think clearly and weigh matters carefully lest they be fooled by deceitful tactics.

V. Abimelech Destroys Shechem (Judg. 9:42-49)

A. Ambush of the Shechemites (9:42-45)

The people of Shechem soon paid dearly for their

error. They permitted the man who could help them to be driven from the city. This allowed Abimelech to do almost as he pleased. He first ambushed the Shechemites as they went to their fields to work one morning. He divided his troops into three companies. When the people reached the fields, he took one company to the gate to prohibit any Shechemites from returning. Then he sent the other two companies to kill those in the fields. Not expecting the attack, the people were defenseless to resist; the result was total slaughter.

With all these people killed, Abimelech attacked the city. He didn't attack until many of the best fighters were removed. Also, by taking the gate quickly that morning, he did so without resistance. Thus he seized the city without great difficulty, slaying the inhabitants and destroying the buildings. Then he even sowed the city "with salt." Salted land is barren and unproductive. Nothing can grow on it. (Cf. Psalm 107:34; "barrenness" is literally "saltiness.")

B. Destruction of the Tower of Shechem (9:46-49)

Within Shechem was a prominent tower and a temple to Baal. Today excavators have uncovered the foundation of a very strong tower on the west side of the ancient city. This probably was a type of palace where the prominent people of Shechem lived. These people were called "lords" (Hebrew). With the rest of the city in ruins, these "lords" moved out of their tower and entered the temple (here called "hold") of "the god Berith" (Baal-berith; cf. 9:4). This temple indicates clearly that the Shechemites worshiped Baal. The temple was likely a strong building, both to protect from attack and to seek help from their god.

When Abimelech heard of this move, he went to "mount Zalmon" (cf. Ps. 68:14; evidently a part of Mount Gerizim), along with his men, to gather green wood to make a fire. They placed the wood next to the temple, setting it on fire. As a result a thousand people died, either from the smoke and fire while within the building or at the hands of Abimelech's men as they tried to escape. The slaughter was complete, making a shambles of the city over which Abimelech had been made king just over three years before.

Certainly the people of Shechem regretted their decision of ever having crowned Abimelech. They had made a terrible mistake. They should have investigated further, examined his motives and seen whether Gideon's other sons intended to rule. But they had acted in haste and now suffered the consequences. Most of these died as a result. Only a few lived to tell the story.

Weigh decisions carefully before making them. Poor choices can lead to sad results.

VI. The Death of Abimelech at Thebez (Judg. 9:50-57)

A. The Death Itself (9:50-55)

Abimelech's next move was to attack the city of Thebez. The people of the city did as the lords of the Shechemites had done, fleeing for refuge to a "strong tower" in the middle of the city. As a result, Abimelech took the city with ease; then he moved against the tower. Again his tactic was to build a fire. However, this time as he came near the door of the tower to place the wood and light the flame, he was a target for those above. Perhaps he had stationed some men to shoot arrows to "cover" those working below; but somehow, by God's intervention, a courageous woman sent a "millstone" crashing down on Abimelech's head, breaking his skull. Millstones were of different sizes, but one used in this way would have been a stone that a single person could use, probably varying from six to fifteen inches in length.

Abimelech had seen that the one who threw the stone was a woman, and he quickly asked his "armourbearer" to strike him with his sword so that it could not be said that a woman had done the deed. The man did as told; and Abimelech died. All his followers returned to their respective homes.

B. A Significant Summation (9:56, 57)

The text closes the sad account with a significant summation: Those involved in the evil acts received a full recompense. The summation states, though in a different way, the truth contained in Galatians 6:7. In respect to Abimelech, read verse 56. Abimelech had thought he served his own interest by his actions, but God saw that vengeance came because of it. In respect to the Shechemites who had cooperated with Abimelech, all their "evil . . . did God render upon their heads," making true for them "the curse of Jotham the son of Jerubbaal." They had been wrong and had to pay.

God has His own way of reprimanding those who oppose Him and His will. When God says, "Vengeance is mine; I will repay," He means what He says. This both warns and comforts the Christian. It warns if he is the one in line for reprimand; it comforts if he is the object of another's evil actions.

Prepare To Answer Intelligently

1. Through whom did Abimelech work to become king?
2. In Jotham's parable, whom did the bramble symbolize?
3. With whom was Zebul working as an ally?
4. How was Zebul able to discredit Gaal in the eyes of the Shechemites?
5. How did Abimelech first attack Shechem, following Gaal's removal from the city?
6. What was Abimelech's next move?
7. Where did the leading people of Shechem retreat?
8. How did Abimelech attack them? With what result?
9. Where was Abimelech killed?
10. How did it happen?

CHAPTER 9

Jephthah and the Ammonites

BIBLE PORTION TO READ: Judges 10:1—12:15

NOW WE REVERT to an account typical of the Book of Judges—oppression from the Ammonites, neighbors of the Midianites whom Gideon had defeated, and deliverance by Jephthah who had been driven from his home because of his illegitimate birth.

I. The Ammonite Oppression (Judg. 10:6-18)
A. The Sin of the Israelites (10:6, 7)

The degree of the Israelites' sin seems to have been getting worse. Not only were the people worshiping "Baalim and Ashtaroth" but the gods of Syria, Zidon, Moab, Ammon and the Philistines (v. 6). Baal worship was still most prominent, but the false deities of other countries were being followed to an increasing degree. The result was that "the anger of the LORD was hot against Israel." Therefore, God sold the people into the hands of the Philistines and Ammonites. The Philistine oppression occurred at the same general time as this to the Ammonites; but it is described in chapters 13-16. It took place west of the Jordan while this to the Ammonites took place on the east.

Greater sin calls for greater punishment. We see this in the double oppression coming from two enemies. Their greater sin shows the wickedness of the human heart even in the face of certain punishment.

B. The Oppression of the Ammonites (10:8, 9, 17, 18)

Since the Ammonites were neighbors of the Midianites, perhaps their rise was partly due to Gideon's defeating the Midianites. They came to power at this time and oppressed the Israelites for eighteen years (10:8). The Israelite area over which they held authority was mainly east of Jordan, but for at least some of the time it extended to the west—in the tribal sections of Judah, Benjamin and Ephraim (10:9).

C. The Repentance of the Israelites (10:10-16)

The story of the Ammonite oppression of Israel is unique in the Book of Judges in that more is said regarding Israel's repentance than in the other accounts. The people seem to have repented in a greater degree. Note the initial show of repentance in verse 10. However, God responded to this—probably through a prophet (vv. 11-14)—by reminding the people of several enemies (Egyptians, Amorites, Ammonites, Philistines, Zidonians, Amalekites and Maonites) from whom He had already delivered them. He indicated that, since these deliverances had not caused them to obey, there was little reason to deliver them again. Instead they should cry to the gods to which they had been giving allegiance and let them deliver them. The people made a fine confession, emphasizing that they had sinned and desired God to deliver them (v. 15). They put away the "strange gods from among them." Then God is said to have been "grieved for the misery of Israel" (v. 16). When the people repented in words and actions, God considered their condition of oppression.

Sin withholds God's blessing. Blessing results only when one repents of and puts away sin.

II. Jephthah Summoned As Deliverer (Judg. 11:1-11)

A. Jephthah the Person (11:1-3)

This time Jephthah of Gilead was the deliverer. He

was born of a harlot. As a result of his illegitimate birth, his half brothers mistreated him and forced him out of the home. Therefore, he could not share in the inheritance rights. He then went to the land of Tob where he gathered a band of men.

B. Summoned As Deliverer Over the Ammonites (11:4-11)

While Jephthah and his band were in Tob, the Ammonites invaded the Israelite lands. The "elders of Gilead" asked Jephthah to lead them against the invaders. Since this request must have come toward the close of the eighteen-year period (Jephthah's resulting attack brought it to an end), these elders first must have tried unsuccessfully to solve their problem other ways. Jephthah seemed to have a reputation as an able military leader. Therefore, they resorted to him.

Jephthah didn't agree at first. He referred to the time of his being driven away. He held these elders and his own half brothers responsible for the earlier action. This implied they had helped expel him or had been sympathetic to the action. The elders' reply didn't counter this implication. They said that it was because of this former wrong that they were asking him to return as their leader (v. 8).

This matter of being "head" caught Jephthah's attention. Would these elders make him head if he succeeded over the Ammonites (v. 9)? The answer was yes; so Jephthah accepted. He was installed as "head and captain" over them (vv. 10, 11). After this Jephthah "uttered all his words before the LORD in Mizpeh" (v. 11), meaning that he stated again—probably before a solemn assembly of Gileadites—the conditions and obligations under which he was accepting the honor conferred on him. The Mizpeh here in view was Jephthah's home (Judg. 11:34).

God vindicates in His own way. Because of Jephthah's improper birth, he had been driven from his hometown unfairly. God righted the wrong by effecting measures that prompted those who had forced him away to recall him and make him head of the community. Always the one who is wronged should look to God for his vindication. God often brings it in unexpected ways.

III. Unfruitful Negotiation (Judg. 11:12-28)

A. First Exchange (11:12, 13)

In his new position of leadership, Jephthah wisely first sought to negotiate peace with the Ammonites. As a military leader, he could have been expected to fight to prove his prowess. Instead, he sent a peace mission to the enemy. He asked the Ammonite king why he had come to fight with Israel. The king replied that it was because the Israelites had first taken away Ammonite property when they had come from Egypt.

B. Jephthah's Threefold Reply (11:14-28)

Jephthah tried unsuccessfully to reason with the Ammonite ruler. Note Jephthah's manner of arguing before the foreign king. He gave three basic reasons to show the king was wrong in his thinking.

1. *The Attack Had Been Provoked (11:14-20)*

Jephthah reviewed the history of the occasion mentioned. Although 300 years had passed (cf. v. 26), Jephthah was knowledgeable of what had transpired. He pointed out that Israel had done all possible to avoid battle with the peoples of the transjordan region, but the fighting resulting in the acquisition of the land had been forced on them. First, Moses had asked Edom for passage through its land. Being refused, he had circuited the land to avoid a war (cf. Num. 20:14-21; 21:5-20). Then Moses had skirted Moab so no quarrel would develop there. Finally Moses had asked Sihon, ruler of the area in question, for passage to the Jordan; but he, too, had refused (cf. Num. 21:21-31). This refusal prompted the fight which brought the land under Israel's control. Therefore, Israel's fighting and winning were not due to her aggressive spirit but to the former inhabitants' lack of cooperation.

2. *The Land Divinely Given (11:21-25)*

Jephthah's second point was that "the LORD God of

Israel" had given the land which the ruler of Ammon now disputed to the Israelites (vv. 21, 22). Therefore, since God had given the land, should a mere human ruler dispute it? Wouldn't Ammon be ready to possess whatever Ammon's god, Chemosh, gave it in similar manner? Therefore, the Israelites were not wrong in possessing what God had given them. Jephthah pointed out that Moab had never sought to reclaim land taken from it at the same time. Ammon should act in the same way (v. 25).

Jephthah did not mean that Chemosh was a real god. He was speaking in language meaningful to this pagan ruler. He did this to make his point.

3. *It Had Been Held Three Hundred Years Already (11:26-28)*

Jephthah said too much time had elapsed since Moses had taken the land to make a claim valid. The Ammonites should have acted sooner.

Jephthah concluded his arguments by asserting that Israel had done no wrong; but Ammon was guilty in attacking Israel. He sent the message to the Ammonite king hoping to change his thinking and actions. But the king paid no attention to the message (v. 28).

Jephthah deserves credit for trying to dissuade the king although he probably knew the attempt would be unsuccessful. Too often Christians give up without trying. One should at least try, not limiting God in what He can or may be willing to do. With Him all things are possible (cf. Jer. 32:27; Luke 1:37).

IV. Victory (Judg. 11:29, 32, 33)

The Ammonite ruler should have listened to Jephthah since he lost the battle.

A. Jephthah Filled by the Holy Spirit (11:29)

The secret of Jephthah's victory is revealed at the beginning of the battle's account. "The Spirit of the LORD came upon" him for this task. In Old Testament days the Holy Spirit came upon people to empower them for tasks (cf. Exod. 31:3; Judg. 13:25; 14:6; etc.).

The key of all victory for God in any day is the Holy Spirit's enabling.

B. The Victorious Conflict (11:29, 32, 33)

With this divine enabling, Jephthah began to prepare for the conflict. In doing so, he traveled through Gilead, Manasseh and back to Mizpeh of Gilead, the place of the impending battle. He must have made this journey in an effort to recruit additional troops. He had his own band, and others had been assembled by the elders at Mizpeh; but he evidently wanted more if possible. Returning to Mizpeh, he made ready to attack. He apparently took the offensive.

One may wonder why the enemy ruler waited so long without attacking while Jephthah made these preparations. He may not have been planning to fight at all. The territory had been his for the past eighteen years (Judg. 10:8); so now he waited to see if this flurry of activity would produce efforts worth his serious attention.

This time God gave His people victory. The people had repented before God and had selected a leader who honored God. This meant victory; for, when God is pleased, there is always victory. Jephthah drove the enemy from the field of battle at Mizpeh and back to their own land, taking twenty Ammonite cities in the process (v. 33). This ended the Ammonite oppression.

V. Jephthah's Strange Vow (Judg. 11:30, 31, 34-40)

A. The Nature of the Vow

Before Jephthah moved against the Ammonites in battle, he made an unusual vow to God. He said that if God would give him victory, he would offer to God whatever came first from the door of his own house to meet him when he returned home. Jephthah made this vow because of his strong desire for victory in the impending struggle. He realized that, if victory were to be gained, God must effect it. This shows dedication to the task assigned by the Gileadite elders and a recognition of dependence on God.

We don't know who or what Jephthah thought would be the first to meet him at his home door; but it was his daughter, an only child. When he saw her, he was greatly distressed (v. 35); he had not counted on it being she. However, he resolved that he would carry out his promise. She agreed with him that he should do so, and preparations were made to that end.

Jephthah has been criticized for making the vow. It has been called rash. On the other hand, we must admire him for it in some respects. He recognized his dependence on God. This is noteworthy in view of his earlier life. He had received unfair treatment in being sent from his home while still young and then had headed a roving band of fighters. He could have become hard and rough, but both his attempt at peaceful negotiation with the enemy and now this vow show that he was really a careful person who sought to do God's will. Then his resolve to carry out the vow, even at great cost, is commendable. Often God's people make resolutions but fail to carry them out, especially if cost is involved. It is better not to make vows at all than to make and then forget them. God expects His children's promises to be kept (cf. Num. 30:1, 2; Ps. 76:11; Eccles. 5:4, 5).

B. The Nature of the Fulfillment

The way in which Jephthah kept the vow has been a subject of debate. It is doubtful that he slew his daughter as a human sacrifice, however. Rather, he probably devoted her to God's service for the rest of her life in perpetual celibacy at the Tabernacle. Several reasons point to this conclusion.

First, for Jephthah to have offered his daughter as a human sacrifice would have been contrary both to Mosaic law (Lev. 18:21; 20:2-5; Deut. 12:31; 18:10) and Israelite practice. Prior to the wicked reigns of Ahaz and Manasseh which occurred much later (2 Kings 16:3; 21:6), there is no record of human sacrifice by Israelites. *Second,* Jephthah respected God and thus wouldn't have gone against the Law and Israelite practice. *Third,* if he had tried to offer his daughter in this way, the Gileadite elders likely would have objected; and if he had done so at the Tabernacle, no priest would have been willing to officiate. *Fourth,* that Jephthah permitted his daughter to bewail her virginity (vv. 37, 38) for two months suits the idea of her soon being devoted to God in perpetual celibacy. *Fifth,* the notice that the daughter "knew no man" (v. 39), given as a result of Jephthah's having carried out the vow, points to her offering being a matter of celibacy. *Sixth,* the pivotal statement of Jephthah in 11:31 that it "shall surely be the LORD's, and I will offer it up for a burnt offering" may be translated with the conjunction "or." This would make the first part a reference to what Jephthah would have done if a human first met him; the second, if an animal.

VI. Jephthah and Ephraim (Judg. 12:1-7)

We noted Gideon's unpleasant encounter with disgruntled Ephraimites in lesson 7 (cf. Judg. 8:1-3). Now they met Jephthah similarly. Ephraimites believed their tribe should lead in all tribal matters. When left out, they were hurt and showed it.

A. Ephraim's Complaint (12:1-3)

This time Ephraim complained that Jephthah had not called on them to help fight the Ammonites. This was almost the same as they had said to Gideon in connection with the Midianites. This time they threatened to burn Jephthah's house. Jephthah reminded them that he had called them to help, but they had refused. Jephthah then asked most pertinently, "Wherefore then are ye come up unto me this day, to fight against me?"

B. Ephraim's Defeat (12:4-7)

The result was that war broke out—not with Israel's enemies, but among the Israelites themselves! Ephraim had crossed the Jordan to Jephthah in Gilead to complain, and the war was fought there. Jephthah's trained men won the battle, then moved quickly to seize fording places of the river where fleeing Ephraimites would have to cross. As each Ephraimite came to the river, Jephthah's men asked him if he were an Ephraimite. If he said "no," he had to say the word "Shibboleth." If he pronounced the "sh" as an "s," they knew he was an Ephraimite and killed him. The Ephraimites pronounced their "sh" different from most or all of the other tribes. Some 42,000 Ephraimites died—a fearful price to pay for their pride.

Pride does not pay. The Ephraimites wanted to be the leading tribe, to have a part in all important occasions among the tribes. But they paid a terrible price for their sin. Pride leads to similar disastrous consequences for God's people in any day.

Prepare To Answer Intelligently

1. In what way were Israelites sinning in greater degree at this time?

2. What greater punishment did God bring as a result?

3. How did Israel's repentance this time compare with that of other times when oppression had come?

4. Why had Jephthah been driven from his home?

5. What promise was made to him to persuade him to return home now?

6. What was the secret of victory in Jephthah's winning over the Ammonites?

7. What vow did Jephthah make to God at this time?

8. Would Jephthah have been right before God if he had killed his daughter as a human sacrifice?

9. What complaint did the Ephraimites make to Jephthah now?

10. What was Ephraim's great sin on this occasion?

CHAPTER 10

Samson the Strong

BIBLE PORTION TO READ: Judges 12:8—14:20

THE INTEREST turns to Samson, known for his great strength. His story occupies four chapters of Judges. We will devote two lessons to these. In this lesson we consider his birth announcement and his first contacts with the Philistines. Also involved is the severe Philistine oppression which lasted forty years. Samson was chosen to deliver Israel from this oppression. This story centers in him rather than in the oppression itself.

I. Samson's Birth Announced Beforehand (Judg. 12:8—13:23)

A. Historical Notes (12:8—13:1)

Samson's story begins with some historical notes. The first concerns the service of three judges who are mentioned only briefly in the sacred record. They were Ibzan, who served in Bethlehem seven years; Elon, who judged in Zebulun ten years and Abdon, who worked in Ephraim eight years. Because the Philistine and Ammonite oppressions occurred at the same general time (Judg. 10:7), these three judgeships (recorded between the accounts of the two oppressions) must have transpired at this time also.

The second historical note concerns the length of the Philistine oppression. It lasted forty years, the longest of all oppressions. Apparently it started at about the same time as that of the Ammonites (cf. Judg. 10:7); but it continued twenty-two years longer. Thus Samson's efforts to offset this oppression of more than twenty years (Judg. 15:20) may have followed Jephthah's judgeship of six years (Judg. 12:7). The combined judgeships of Ibzan, Elon and Abdon could have overlapped both a few years.

B. Samson's Parents (13:2)

Samson's father was Manoah, a member of the tribe of Dan. A sadness existed in Manoah's marriage: His wife, whose name is not given, was barren.

C. The Birth Announcement by the Angel of the Lord (13:3-8)

Samson was highly honored in having his birth foreannounced by a heavenly messenger, putting him in a class with Isaac (Gen. 18:9-15) and John the Baptist (Luke 1:11-20).

1. *The Appearance to Manoah's Wife (13:3-5)*

The heavenly messenger was the Angel of the Lord, the Second Person of the Godhead in preincarnate form, the same as appeared to Gideon in chapter 6 (cf. lesson 5 for discussion). The Angel appeared to Manoah's wife when she was alone. He told her that, though she had been barren, she would bear a son. As she anticipated the birth, she should not drink wine or strong drink nor eat any unclean food because the one to be born would be a Nazarite to God. A Nazarite was one who had taken a vow to separate himself wholly to God, involving abstinence from strong drink, unclean food and cutting one's hair (cf. Num. 6:1-21). Further, this son would be one to "begin to deliver Israel out of the hand of the Philistines." The intended thought in connecting these two ideas is that Samson's enabling to effect this deliverance would come in view of his Nazarite manner of life in which the mother should share before he was born. The idea that Samson would only "begin" to deliver Israel is probably that he would only initiate minor quarrels with the Philistines, such as he did (confusing them, upsetting their plans of expansion and making them see the greatness of Israel's God), rather than raise an army to effect a full deliverance.

2. *The Information Conveyed to Manoah (13:6-8)*

In great excitement, Manoah's wife told her husband the news. She referred to the messenger as a "man of God." She had not realized the Angel's true identity, though she spoke of him as having "the countenance of an angel of God, very terrible [fearful]." She knew the person was to be feared and respected. She related the message he had given her; then Manoah asked God that this one be permitted to come again so he could receive more information. He, too, was excited. A son was promised, one who would serve to deliver Israel!

D. Second Appearance of the Angel (13:9-23)

1. *The Repeated Instructions (13:9-14)*

God heard Manoah's prayer and again sent the Angel when the woman was alone in the field. She quickly summoned her husband. Manoah's first words to the Angel were to ask if He was the One Who had come to his wife earlier. Learning that He was, he asked, "How shall we order the child, and how shall we do unto him?" (Literally, "What will be the manner of the child, and what will he do?") The Angel repeated the instructions already given to the wife—that she should neither drink strong drink nor eat anything unclean. Although Manoah wanted to know about the child, what he would be like and how he would deliver Israel, the Angel only repeated what the mother should do in anticipation of the birth. Thus the Angel said in effect, "One thing at a time, Manoah. Now it is enough for you to know only what to do before the birth. When that has occurred, you will learn about the boy himself."

Christians today are much like Manoah, wanting to

know the end from the beginning before they start to do what God orders. But God often wants them simply to trust Him for succeeding steps by taking the first one without knowing what the others will be.

2. *The Credential of Authority (13:15-21)*

Next Manoah asked the Angel, Whose identity he still did not know, to wait and dine with him and his wife. No doubt he wanted to show hospitality to one who was important, and he also wished to have time to learn more information concerning this son. The Angel responded that he would not eat food, even if it were prepared; but if Manoah wanted to offer a burnt offering, he should do this, offering it to the Lord. The added note that "Manoah knew not that he was an angel of the LORD" not only meant that he was ignorant of this fact, but also promised that, when he offered this sacrifice, he would learn of it. The offering became proof of the Angel's identity and authority.

Next Manoah asked the Angel's name. The Angel mildly rebuked him, asking, "Why askest thou thus after my name, seeing it is secret [wonderful]?" The Angel gave Manoah some information; namely, that his name was a "wonderful" one.

Manoah proceeded as the Angel had suggested. He prepared "a kid" as a burnt offering and sacrificed it along with a "meat offering" (meal offering, which was always to accompany a burnt offering—Lev. 2:1-16). When he did this, "the angel did wonderously." The same word is used here (only in verbal form) as in verse 18. The significance is that the Angel acted in a way to give evidence that His identity did carry a "wonderful" name. The next verse reveals the manner in which he "did wonderously." He "ascended in the flame of the altar." As Manoah and his wife watched, the Angel suddenly rose from the earth, moving upward in the smoke of the sacrifice. The two mortals immediately fell prostrate to the earth. When they realized that the Angel was gone to return no more, they recognized that he was the "angel of the LORD."

3. Manoah's Reaction (13:22, 23)

Manoah's reaction to this experience was similar to Gideon's. He thought he and his wife would die because they had seen God (cf. Judg. 6:22, 23). As noted previously, a glimpse of God regularly brings a sense of fear and shame, for the person realizes his own unworthiness as compared to God's perfect righteousness (cf. Job 42:5, 6; Isa. 6:5). Manoah's wife reminded him that, if God had intended to kill them, He would neither have accepted the offering given, let them see what they had nor hear the good news revealed. She seems to have had greater presence of mind than her husband. Out of respect and awe, it was appropriate for Manoah to fear God but not to expect death. His wife recognized this and helped him in his thinking. She is to be commended for this. Husbands and wives always are to help each other.

E. Significance

Why was the announcement of Samson's birth given beforehand? No other judge was distinguished in this way. Why was Samson so honored? The question becomes more pertinent and difficult to answer when one considers the serious failures in Samson's life. He was unable to resist women's charms. Because he later fell prey to the Philistine woman Delilah (Judg. 16:4-21), he lost his divinely given strength and became a slave in a Philistine prison.

One should not think of Samson too critically. He is said to have been empowered especially by the Holy Spirit no less than four times (Judg. 13:25; 14:6, 19; 15:14) which is three more than any of the other judges. Also God miraculously provided water when he was thirsty (15:19). Both these matters were carried out during his life when his weakness was already known. This indicated God's continued blessing in spite of the sin.

Note also that Samson judged Israel for twenty years (Judg. 15:20), and no sinful episodes regarding him are recorded during most of the time. Most of his life may have been well-ordered and God-pleasing. Perhaps this is why he was included in the Hebrews honor roll of faith (11:32). Samson didn't fail completely; he accomplished some meaningful things for God.

However, it is certain that Samson's potential, in view of this remarkable foreannouncement and God's continued gracious provisions, was far more than he accomplished. He undoubtedly could have accomplished many more things had he kept his life pure and fully dedicated to God. Thus he provides a warning that sin does not pay. Life and service are spoiled when one lets sin enter his life.

II. Samson's First Exploits (Judg. 13:24—14:20)

A. Birth (13:24, 25)

In due time Manoah's wife gave birth to the one thus promised. He was called Samson. We assume that his mother had followed the Angel's instructions in not drinking strong drink or eating unclean food. Thus Samson was a true Nazarite, even from the time of his conception. As years passed, the boy grew and "the LORD blessed him," likely in the form of a fine appearance, a healthy body and a good reputation.

The "Spirit of the LORD" began to move him. The area where this occurred was "the camp of Dan between Zorah and Eshtaol," his home territory. Here God's Spirit came on Samson to give him his unusual strength and incline his heart toward God's work for him.

The Holy Spirit works through believers' lives today. He indwells them and seeks to be dominant in their lives. When Christians disobey, God's work through them is hindered (quenched, 1 Thess. 5:19). Obedient lives permit His work to flourish.

B. Enamored by a Philistine Girl (14:1-4)

As Samson grew older, his activities took him into Philistine territory. His parents' home bordered on this foreign area. Once while in Timnath, Samson saw a young Philistine lady who appealed to him. He told his parents he wanted to marry her and asked them to arrange the wedding. They objected because such marriages were forbidden to Israelites (Deut. 7:3, 4). But Samson insisted, and the parents complied. Verse 4 signifies that something more than a wedding was intended (by God, and perhaps Samson understood this in some measure too) in the arrangement; namely, an "occasion against the Philistines" when a quarrel might be provoked. God assigned Samson the task to "begin" to deliver from the Philistines, and one way to begin was through such occasions of quarrel. God often uses occasions which He permits in Christians' lives to accomplish some purpose that is not obvious or generally recognized.

C. Samson and the Lion (14:5-9)

1. *Killing the Lion (14:5-7)*

Samson's encounter with the lion is probably the best-known episode from his life. He and his parents were on their way to Timnath to arrange for the wedding. On the way "a young lion roared against him," and he stopped long enough to kill it. The "Spirit of the LORD" again "came mightily upon him"; and he was able to rend the lion as if it were a young goat. He did this with his bare hands alone, having no instrument. David, when a shepherd, and the hero Benaiah also slew lions (1 Sam. 17:34, 35; 2 Sam. 23:20). Samson's special strength here, as enabled by the Holy Spirit, was shown in his being able to rend the animal as he killed it. When the deed was done, he didn't even tell his parents of it (somehow they were not present at the time); but he continued his walk to Timnath as if nothing had happened.

This story gives the background for Samson's riddle to the wedding guests. That God sent His Spirit to give special enabling for the task reinforces the thought that the quarrel instituted as a result of it was according to God's will. God sent the Spirit in this way only when there was good reason. Here it was to initiate an occasion to fight the Philistines.

2. *The Swarm of Bees (14:8, 9)*

Sometime later, when he was on the way to Timnath for the wedding, Samson detoured to look at the lion he had killed. To his surprise he found a swarm of bees and honey already made within the carcass. He ate some of the honey and, when he caught up to his father and mother, gave some to them also. He didn't tell them of the incident, however, evidently planning to formulate a riddle to use with the Philistines and not wanting anyone to know about it.

D. Samson's Wedding and Riddle (14:10-18)

1. *The Wedding (14:10, 11)*

When he reached Timnath, Samson "made there a feast" which was to last seven days (v. 17). The young man was the one to put on the feast, arranging for it and probably financing it. It normally took place at the groom's home; but in this case, perhaps because the bride was of another people, it was held at the bride's home.

Another custom was that the groom should be attended by several young men. However, Samson hadn't brought any with him; therefore, the Philistines provided some from their own number. The words "when they saw him" (v. 11) suggest their seeing him without being accompanied by the expected companions. Thirty young Philistines made up the group. They were to be Samson's companions for the seven days to help him enjoy the occasion to the full.

2. *The Riddle (14:12-18)*

Samson initiated the relationship with the thirty by telling the riddle that had come to mind. He said that if they could guess the answer within the seven days of the feast, he would give each a change of "sheets" and "garments." The "sheets" referred to the flowing linen garment worn next to the body. The "garments" were placed over these. This was a complete change of clothing. If they could not guess it, they would each have to give him a similar change.

The riddle was, "Out of the eater came forth meat, and out of the strong came forth sweetness." The men were to guess the identity of the "eater" and the "strong" and the source of the "sweetness."

The men accepted the challenge, but for six days they couldn't guess the answer. On the seventh day they forced Samson's bride to get the answer for them, threatening to burn her and her father's house if she didn't. She agreed to the demand. With many tears she persuaded Samson to tell her the answer. Verse 17 indicates that she had been trying for six days; but on the seventh, in view of the young men's threat, she urged more insistently. When she obtained the information, she told the young men. They brought the answer to Samson, winning the contest. Samson knew what had happened and regretted telling his bride.

Many men, including Christians, have had their lives and service ruined because of an improper relationship with women. They have permitted themselves to fall in love with those who were improper companions or didn't requite their love and then have been led into other evil as a result. Men and women must be extremely careful as to the persons with whom they allow themselves to associate and fall in love.

This same basic area of sin continued to be the predominant one in Samson's life. Satan, knowing a Christian's basic area of weakness, continually centers his attention on that area. The Christian should realize this and trust God the more for victory over it. An area of weakness is no excuse for sin. Christ provides all that is necessary for victory over it (cf. Rom. 6:11-14).

E. Samson and Thirty Philistines (14:19, 20)

Samson's way of paying his debt to these thirty men was to kill thirty other Philistines and take their garments. He did not do this at Timnath but went to Ashkelon, one of the five main Philistine cities. Once more the "Spirit of the LORD" came upon him for the task, and he brought the garments back and gave them to the thirty. Then he left his young bride, angry at her and the young men, and returned to his father's house. His bride was given as wife to a companion who had received a set of the garments.

Thus ended Samson's first encounter with the Philistines. He had accomplished something in regard to his God-assigned task. His being able to pay his debt as he did, taking the lives of thirty Philistines, must have become known among the enemy nation; and the exploit would have caused amazement. This was only a beginning, but the Philistines would notice this Israelite. When he did other exploits, they would ponder the reason. Israel's God must be remarkable to empower one man in this way.

The regrettable aspect is that this power had to be shown in connection with Samson's weakness. The Philistines would have realized this. Delilah's later attempts to persuade him to tell her the secret of his strength may well have been suggested because he had succumbed to the charms of this bride. Samson could have been more effective in his assigned task if he had conquered this area of sin in his life.

Prepare To Answer Intelligently

1. What does being a Nazarite mean?
2. How did the Angel of the Lord show His identity?
3. What was Manoah's reaction to this miracle?
4. What was the main area of sin in Samson's life?
5. Where did the Philistine girl live that Samson wanted to marry?
6. Was Samson right or wrong in wanting to marry her? Why?
7. What is the meaning of the phrase in Judges 14:4, "an occasion against the Philistines"?
8. To whom did Samson propound his riddle?
9. How did these people finally procure the answer?
10. How did Samson pay the debt he thus incurred?

CHAPTER 11

Samson's Success and Failure

BIBLE PORTION TO READ: Judges 15:1—16:31

THIS CONTINUES the account of Samson. Previously we noticed only his first encounter with the Philistines. Here his remaining encounters with the enemy are noticed. These fall either at the beginning or end of his twenty years of judgeship.

I. Wheat Harvest Events (Judg. 15:1-19)

The second series of events fall at the time of wheat harvest, within a year of the first events.

A. The Return to Timnath (15:1-3)

In time Samson's anger at his bride and the Philistines abated, and he went to her again. This was the first wheat harvest after the wedding; so Samson's anger continued for less than a year.

He took "a kid" with him as a present and came to the house, expecting to go to her room. The father stopped him, saying that she had been given to one of his companions. The father sought to interest Samson in her younger sister, but Samson became angry at this further wrong. He planned revenge, reasoning that what he would do to them would be less serious than what they had done to him. In view of the enormity of what he now did, however, he must have seen the wrong done to him as representing all the wrong the Philistines had done in oppressing Israel.

Vindictiveness is not normally pleasing to God. Christians aren't to plot revenge for wrongs done to them (Rom. 12:19). However, in Samson's case vengeance seems to have been part of God's assignment. He should become involved in quarrels and bring appropriate reprisals so the Philistines would be disrupted in their offensives against Israel and be caused to respect Israel's God Who could empower a man this way.

B. Revenge with the Foxes (15:4-6)

Samson planned and effected the following as his way of retaliation: He *caught* three hundred foxes (or possibly jackals), tied firebrands to pairs of them joined by their tails and released them to burn the Philistine grain, vineyards and oliveyards. Tying the animals in pairs, with flaming torches between them, insured that they would run wildly, setting fire to a wide area and almost everything in that area.

The Philistines were alarmed. A nation lives on its agricultural produce, and their crops were going up in smoke. After consultations, it was revealed that Samson was responsible. Then, since they could not lay hands on him, they went to his wife's home and burned both her and her father. This girl, who had earlier avoided a similar fate at the hands of Samson's companions (14:15), was now killed. God has His way of bringing reprisal, and He brings it as He sees best. The girl had tried to preserve herself by betraying her husband, but her sin caught up with her.

C. Revenge by Slaughter (15:7, 8)

Hearing of the Philistines' action, Samson resolved to retaliate. It seems he still loved his wife. His words in verse 7 mean that he would not cease in retaliatory action until this killing had been avenged.

He made a "great slaughter," smiting the enemy "hip and thigh." This was a severe slaughter. We don't know the exact number killed, but it must have been large. It probably occurred around Timnath, since the people who killed the girl and her father lived there.

In view of these violent reprisals, consider the effect on the Philistines. It would have been difficult to lose crops and the lives of so many people. However, they would have marveled at the man who had been responsible for both. What ability was shown in catching fast-moving animals and tying them in pairs! What strength and skill were demonstrated in slaughtering so many people at one time! Because people of the day always related such matters to the god the person worshiped, the Philistines must have admired Samson's God Who enabled him.

D. Disappointment with Judaeans (15:8-13)

1. *Philistines Attempt To Capture Samson (15:8-10)*

After the slaughter of the Philistines, Samson retreated from the scene of conflict and went to "the top of the rock Etam." Likely from here he could view any pursuit. In view of verse 7, he wanted to cease the matter of reprisal; but he wasn't sure the Philistines would quit. Therefore, he wouldn't go to his home, for they might come and burn it as they had his wife and father-in-law. Instead, he would watch.

The Philistines did pursue to a place called Lehi, probably near Zorah, Samson's home city. It was in Judaean territory, for Judaeans came to them to ask what was wanted. They answered, "To bind Samson are we come up, to do to him as he hath done to us."

2. *Delivered Over by the Judaeans (15:11-13)*

At this, three thousand Judaeans came to take Samson and deliver him to the Philistines. They knew where he was, and probably the place was not far from Lehi where the Philistines were. Perhaps the Philistines had purposely come to scare these Judaeans into doing what they did. In this way the Philistines would not have to risk capturing Samson themselves.

The words of these fellow Judaeans in verse 11 must have dismayed Samson. They rebuked him for challenging the Philistines, saying he was bringing trouble on them. They should have rejoiced that he had courage to make such a challenge, then volunteered their services to free themselves from foreign domination. Instead, they were ready to be dominated and to oppose any who dared to try for change.

Many Christians today are like these Judaeans. They see the enemy's strength, believe it is too great to oppose and live defeated lives. But God wants a victorious people, not defeated. He wants triumphant, resourceful, courageous soldiers, involved in and eager for battle.

Samson, not wanting to retaliate against his own people, let them bind him. This was admirable. The people deserved to suffer for this action, but he chose not to resist. He didn't want to hurt Judaeans.

Here is a lesson for Christians today. Some spend more time fighting among themselves than with the true enemy. They need all their energy to combat Satan.

E. Samson Kills One Thousand Philistines (15:14-17)

When he was delivered bound to the Philistines, Samson experienced his greatest moment of triumph prior to his day of death. The "Spirit of the LORD came mightily upon him" for the fourth time. First he broke the two ropes as if they were flax burnt with fire; then he killed no less than a thousand of the enemy.

The Philistines had rejoiced when Samson was delivered by the Judaeans. They had come to get him; and now his own people were bringing him, trussed and helpless. This rejoicing was short lived, however. Suddenly, when the Judaeans were safely removed, Samson broke the ropes and started the slaughter of the Philistines, using a "new jawbone of an ass." That he killed so many, making the dead as "heaps upon heaps" (v. 16), suggests that this was accomplished as the Philistines fled. Imagine the large host turning and running for their lives. Fleeing in this way, they became more easy to kill. Thus Samson pursued, striking one after the other. He did not cease until one thousand bodies lay strewn along the way. What a display of power and ability to impress the Philistines!

F. A Gracious Provision (15:18, 19)

After the enormous exertion of slaying so many men, Samson was thirsty. Therefore, he asked God for water to drink, having faith that God could and would do so. Verse 18 shows his reasoning. This went beyond mere physical satisfaction: If he should die of thirst now, he would fall into the hands of the Philistines. This would spoil the effect of the accomplishment.

God doesn't normally provide a miracle just to quench thirst. Therefore, note three matters regarding this incident. *First,* Samson was apparently in danger of dying if he didn't get water quickly. Then the Philistines could take him. *Second,* Samson exercised great faith in God to ask for such a miracle, showing he was a man of faith as indicated in Hebrews 11:32. And *third,* God had been pleased with Samson's actions in these recent events, especially in respect to the Judaeans and the slaughter of the enemy. God provides when His own conduct themselves properly before Him.

II. Twenty-Year Judgeship (Judg. 15:20)

This slaughter of the Philistines brought the earlier contacts with the Philistines to a close. Samson had dealt them a terrible blow, and they weren't going to retaliate further. Samson had sufficiently fulfilled God's assignment and could devote himself to matters of judging for a time.

In keeping with Judges 15:20 and 16:31, twenty years had now elapsed in which Samson was occupied with the service of judging the Israelites. He may have dwelt in Hebron. At least 16:3 reads that he carried the Gaza gate "to the top of an hill that is before Hebron," implying that he headed toward Hebron as his home city. Perhaps Zorah wouldn't accept him as judge as is suggested by their delivering him to the Philistines.

III. Samson's Downfall and Death (Judg. 16:1-31)

A. Samson at Gaza (16:1-3)

Samson went to Gaza—likely near the close of his judgeship at Hebron. Again he fell victim to his passionate nature and went to see a harlot. The Philistines, remembering him, noted him enter the harlot's place and planned to trap and kill him the following morning when they thought he would leave.

Samson left at midnight, breaking the lock and carrying the gate—with the posts and locking bar—away. The Philistines probably saw him, for they would have been watching; but they wouldn't try to stop him when he showed this kind of herculean strength. Thus Samson left unmolested, taking the gate to the top of a hill facing Hebron. He left it there and likely continued on to Hebron.

Again Samson displayed his great strength before this people. The sad part of the story is that he did it only after showing that he still had his passionate nature. God's grace to him in maintaining his superhuman strength spared him from death this time, but it wouldn't do so at a future time.

B. Samson and Delilah (16:4-20)

1. *The Setting (16:4, 5)*

Samson's experience with Delilah came at the close of his life. Somehow he became infatuated with another Philistine woman. If he still resided at Hebron, which is likely, he had more than twenty miles to go; for she lived in the "valley of Sorek." He stayed there some time although no marriage was involved. Learning of these visits, the Philistine leaders came to Delilah, promising that each one would give her "eleven hundred pieces of silver" (at least seventy-five cents for each piece), if she would entice Samson to tell the secret of his strength so she could tell them. Clearly she didn't requite Samson's love and so agreed.

2. *The Enticement (16:6-17)*

Scheming women hold power over infatuated men. Men, otherwise strong, become weak before such a person. This was Samson, a giant in physical strength but helpless in Delilah's hands. For a time he resisted her but then could refuse no longer. Three times he lied to her as she pleaded for the secret of his strength. First he told her that he would be weak normally if he were bound with "seven green withs" (v. 7—pieces of catgut or animal sinew). Then he told her this would be true if he were bound with "new ropes that never were occupied" (v. 11). Finally he said it would be true if his hair, evidently divided into seven locks, was woven together with a web and fastened with a pin (v. 13). Delilah followed through on each suggestion, but still Samson didn't recognize her true nature and intent. This shows the seriousness of uncontrolled sensual appetite.

If a person with the blessings of life that Samson enjoyed and with God's supernatural presence continually endowing him with strength could fall so low in the power of an evil woman, it behooves every Christian to take heed. Sensual sins are extremely difficult to overcome. Because they can greatly harm one's life and service, every Christian should appropriate God's strength to gain that victory.

3. *The Fall (16:18-20)*

Samson told Delilah the truth. He said he had been a Nazarite from his mother's womb; thus his hair had remained unshaven. If his hair was cut off, he would be weak as other men. Delilah knew he was telling the truth; so she called the Philistine leaders to tell them. They came and brought the promised money with them. Then Delilah cut Samson's hair. The result was weakness and an inability to resist being taken by the Philistines. Samson's sin had caught up with him just as everyone's does.

C. The Imprisonment (16:21, 22)

Samson was now taken away to a prison in Gaza. Helpless before his captors, his eyes were gouged out and he was bound with brass chains. In this condition of complete humiliation, he was made to grind grain at a prison mill. Whereas before he had been free, strong and able to kill hundreds by himself, now he was chained, weak and compelled to do a menial task. He had lost the presence of God with him. When he had fallen before the wiles of a woman and his hair had been cut, God's presence and power had left (cf. v. 20). Then the suffering and trouble began.

As long as God's children of any day enjoy His presence and blessing, they are strong and able in God's work; but when that presence and blessing leave, suffering and trouble come.

The most tragic part was the harm that Samson's imprisonment brought to Israel and God. Because of Samson, the Philistines had looked quite differently at their neighbor foe whom they had overrun for some years with considerable ease. This representative was stronger and more capable than any of their heroes. Also, Israel's God was made greater in their eyes because their own gods had never empowered a man like Samson. However, now he had been conquered; thus the Philistines felt their gods were more powerful after all. Also, they could again think seriously of aggression against Israel. Today the matter is serious enough for a child of God when he falls into sin; but God's work and His name suffer more greatly.

D. Victory in Death (16:23-31)

In time Samson's hair grew long, and his recognition of his folly increased. As a result God's presence and strength returned. He had an opportunity to use that renewed strength at a Philistine feast to Dagon, their main deity. A great host had gathered at the central temple. Although the feast was to Dagon, they were celebrating Samson's capture. Thus not many weeks had elapsed since his capture. Then they called for Samson himself to be led in.

Samson was brought to the center of the temple so all could see him. At first the crowd mocked and made sport of him. Samson asked to be led to the two central supporting pillars of the building. There he called on God to restore his strength "this once" so that he could be avenged of the Philistines for his two eyes. Then, pushing with that strength restored, he was able to make the pillars fall; and the building collapsed. More than three thousand people had been "upon the roof" alone, and these were pitched headlong among the many on the lower floor. The death toll was enormous. Samson also died, but the people he killed through his death were more than all he had killed during his life.

In this closing moment of triumph, God graciously permitted Samson to make up a little for the foolishness that had brought his fall. However, nothing could offset the harm he had done. His sinfulness had been so serious that the total effect of his work for God had been curtailed. He is a prime example of one who had great potential and opportunity but who lost much because of grievous sin in his life.

Prepare To Answer Intelligently

1. What wrong did Samson avenge by using 300 foxes?
2. What wrong did he avenge by committing a "great slaughter" among the Philistines?
3. Who came to bind Samson at the top of rock Etam?
4. What was Samson's request of them?
5. How many Philistines did he kill at Lehi?
6. What gracious provision did God give to Samson after this?
7. What did the Philistine leaders promise Delilah?
8. What three "lies" did Samson tell Delilah at first?
9. What happened to Samson when his hair was cut?
10. At what feast did Samson gain revenge over the Philistines?
11. What did Samson do there to bring his vengeance?

CHAPTER 12

Micah and the Danites

BIBLE PORTION TO READ: Judges 17:1—18:31

THE SUBJECT MATTER of this lesson and next differs from that of the others. No longer is the interest with a judge or a period of oppression from which he brought deliverance. Rather, it is with two representative stories illustrating the sin the people committed. As has been mentioned, sin brought the oppressions. Here we have the kinds of sins which brought them. Both occurred early in the Period of the Judges, probably before sin became as serious or extensive as it did later.

I. The Sin of Micah (Judg. 17:1-13)

The first story concerns an Ephraimite named Micah and the movement of the Danites to new territory. These two stories are distinct from each other; but they become intertwined so that they really form one.

A. The Stolen Money (17:1-3)

1. *The Time Involved*

First note when this story occurred. Two matters indicate that it came early in the period. The first comes from the Book of Joshua which mentions the movement of the Danites (19:47) and which was written at a time when Rahab the harlot still lived (Josh. 6:25). The other follows in view of the reason for the move. As

Joshua 19:47 indicates, the Danites found their territory too small for them. (It wouldn't have been if they had occupied all; cf. Judges 1:34 and the first lesson.) Therefore, they wanted more. This desire obviously arose shortly after the allotment. Thus they likely moved in this way soon after.

2. *Micah and His Mother*

A man named Micah (not the prophet who wrote the book) lived with his mother in "mount Ephraim." He had stolen 1,100 shekels of silver (a shekel was worth at least 75 cents) from his mother, and the story opens with his confessing the fact to her. She responded by bestowing a blessing on him and said that she intended the money to be given to God in behalf of her son anyway. "A graven image and a molten image" were to be made from it. Micah restored the money to her to do as she intended.

Several sins were here involved. First, Micah stole from his mother. His confession did not excuse him. In fact, he probably confessed because of her previous curse on whoever had done it (v. 2), making him fear what might happen to him. Micah thus broke the Eighth Commandment (Exod. 20:15). Second, the mother sinned in not rebuking her son. Instead, she blessed him as though his deed were not wrong. Discipline—appropriate and controlled—is necessary so children will fully realize their sin. A third sin was that the mother desired to make images of God, thus breaking the Second Commandment (Exod. 20:4).

B. Micah's Private Sanctuary (17:4-6)

1. *The Story*

With the money Micah restored, the mother took 200 shekels and gave them to the image maker to form a "graven image" and a "molten image." Why she used only 200 of the total 1,100 shekels is not explained. Perhaps only 200 were required to make the images. The images were placed in a "house of gods." He also made an "ephod," a replica of the official apron-like garment worn by the high priest, symbolizing his authority for hearing from God on the people's behalf. Gideon had made one of these and had brought God's displeasure on him. Further, Micah made "teraphim" (likely small images of gods, Gen. 31:19) to go along with the larger gods made from the 200 shekels of silver. Then he consecrated one of his sons as priest. Thus Micah established his own sanctuary of worship.

2. *The Serious Sins*

All this was done, according to the mother's words, "unto the LORD" (v. 3), as a way to worship Israel's God. The intention to worship God rather than Baal was good, but it was wrong to do it this way. In fact, everything about Micah's sanctuary was wrong.

First, the idea of having such a private place of worship was a sin. God had designated the Tabernacle at Shiloh as the only such place (cf. Deut. 12:5, 6, 11, 14). People were to go *there* with their sacrifices. People should pray and have private devotions at home but not their own temples for sacrifices. All were to go to the central sanctuary.

Second, the making of the gods was sin. As just noted, God had directed that no images of Him be made.

Third, it was wrong to make the ephod. The high priest was the only person to wear this garment.

Fourth, to make the teraphim, the smaller household-type gods, was a sin.

Fifth, making Micah's son a priest was sin. God had set aside the tribe of Levi to serve in the priestly capacity. Micah's family were Ephraimites. Micah had no right to make his own son a priest.

Verse 6 is significant for being included at this point. It is duplicated in the last verse of the book (21:25) as a sort of summary statement for the whole book; but here it accounts for Micah's sinful procedure. Men in Israel were doing as they wished, each determining for himself what was right. That the verse is given here, when it was to be included in a general sense at the close of the book, suggests that Micah's sinful actions were especially shocking.

In passing it may be said that liberal expositors understand Micah's action to have been quite the norm for the day. However, his actions were *not* normative. Rather, they were sinful and contrary to the Law. The Law had been revealed through Moses, and Micah here directly disobeyed the clear injunctions set forth.

C. An Errant Levite (17:7-13)

1. *The Man (17:7, 8)*

Another figure, a young Levite from Bethlehem of Judah, stepped into the story. His home being in Bethlehem is significant, for it should not have been. That is, all priests and Levites had been assigned specific cities in which to live. These were called Levitic cities (Num. 35:1-8; Josh. 21:1-41). Bethlehem was not among them. Therefore, this man's living in Bethlehem shows that he had already been out of God's will. He must have left the city to which he had originally been assigned to reside in Bethlehem. His leaving Bethlehem and moving shows that Bethlehem didn't suit him. Once more he was looking for greener pastures as he came to Micah's house.

Like this wandering Levite, many Christians today are never satisfied with the place God has placed them. He has a place for each of His children to be and to serve, but often His children don't want to be there. Things become disagreeable to them; they look elsewhere and move. One should realize that no matter where he is, things will not be perfect. Every Christian should desire to be in God's place for him. Here God enables one to cope with and overcome the disagreeable aspects.

2. *The Agreement with Micah (17:9-12)*

The wandering Levite and Micah met, and Micah asked him, "Whence comest thou?" The man answered that he was from Bethlehem and that he was going wherever he could find a suitable place. This interested Micah, and he offered him the position as his private priest. He had made his son priest, but he believed that his sanctuary would be improved if this Levite would do the work. Accordingly, he made him an offer: ten shekels a year as wages (less than ten dollars), a suit of clothing and board. Certainly a place to sleep was also included, something the young man could take for granted. The Levite agreed, took up residence at Micah's home and became so popular that he was as one of Micah's sons.

This, too, was serious sin—trying to procure the services of a private priest. God had instituted the priesthood for all, not for specific people. The Levite sinned in seeking such a position and in accepting it when offered. He was an opportunist, looking for the best situation. However, priests and Levites were not intended to be opportunists. They were to live in designated cities and do assigned work.

3. *Micah's False Satisfaction (17:13)*

When Micah had completed this arrangement, he felt personal satisfaction. He believed the Lord would do him good since he had a Levite as priest instead of his son. Micah's confused thinking reveals certain matters. First, he believed in the true God, the Lord of Israel. Second, he wished to be in God's good favor. Third, he recognized that having his own son as priest was not right. Fourth, he knew God had designated Levites to be the priests. And fifth, he did not know— or at least did not follow the knowledge if he had it— that priests should serve at only the central sanctuary. Micah may have been sincere, but he was wrong. He may not have been correctly instructed in these matters. Since his mother made false images, she probably had not taught him aright. Priests and Levites of the day were supposed to do such teaching (cf. Deut. 33:10), along with parents; but quite possibly they were not doing their job properly. Micah may have had an excuse; but there was none for the general sinfulness of the people which would result in such conduct on the part of any person. God had reason to punish a people who did not obey Him.

II. The Sin of the Danites (Judg. 18:1-31)

At the time Micah was establishing his own sanctuary, the Danites were discontented. They, too, wanted to move. They had found difficulty occupying all the land they had been allotted, and they wished to find more land so many of them could move there. This desire was sinful. God had given them their allotment to occupy, not to leave.

A. A Search for New Land (18:1, 2)

The indication (v. 1) that all the inheritance of the Danites had not fallen to the people doesn't mean that the other tribes had deprived them of it. They simply had not driven out the Canaanites from the land assigned them (cf. Judg. 1:34). Needing more land (Dan was a large tribe, second to Judah; cf. Num. 26:42, 43), a committee of five men was sent to find a new area. They left from Zorah (Samson's birthplace) and Eshtaol to make the search.

Apparently discontent caused the Levite to want to move. The Danites' problem was an unwillingness to work. Both factors cause today's Christians to want to move. Many of God's people are lazy in God's work. But work is a part of the assignment when God places a person in a particular location. He wants that one to get busy and carry out the task at hand.

B. The Visit to Micah's Private Sanctuary (18:3-6)

As the committee of five searched for new land, they came to Micah's home in Ephraim. There they met the young Levite and asked him about himself. When he had told them his story, they requested him to ask God if their going would be prosperous. They thought that if this man was a priest, as he said, he should be able to inquire of God for them. The young man didn't refuse the request but answered in the words of Judges 18:6. He said their intended way was known to God, and He was pleased with it. No doubt the young man had inquired by means of the ephod before replying.

Once again we see the presence of sin. The committee was wrong in asking the Levite to inquire of God, and the Levite was wrong in bringing an answer. God had instituted a way to inquire of Him. The high priest, who alone was to wear the authenticating ephod, could bring requests to God, using the Urim and Thummim which were kept in the linen breastplate of the ephod (cf. Exod. 28:6-31). Neither an ordinary priest nor a Levite should attempt to do this. In this way God safeguarded the making of an inquiry so that it would not be used improperly or lightly. That these Danites inquired and the Levite was willing to answer shows the influence of pagan thinking. The Canaanites and other neighbors inquired of many of their priests. However, Israel was not to do so. Certainly the answer the young Levite gave was not received from God.

C. Discovery of Laish (18:7-11)

After the five-man committee left the young Levite, they went north through Naphtali, arriving in Laish some twenty-five miles north of the Sea of Galilee at the foot of Mount Hermon. The city was quite alone. Zidon, evidently its natural protector, was too far away to help them if they were attacked. They thought the city was the one for which they were looking; so they returned to report to their people.

They told those who had sent them of their discovery and described it as a "very good" land. They said the people were overconfident and could be easily defeated. They felt the area was "large" enough and would provide good living conditions. They urged the people to arise and take the land. "Six hundred men appointed with weapons of war" arose to do as urged.

Why were the Danites suddenly willing to fight the people of Laish for this land when they had not been willing to fight the Canaanites for theirs? Undoubtedly they believed that fighting for Laish would be easier. We reach this conclusion from verse 7 and from their report concerning conditions which would make the fighting comparatively easy. They were willing to travel over a hundred miles to fight complete strangers, to seize land God had not allotted.

D. Robbery of Micah's Sanctuary (18:12-26)
1. *The March There (18:12-15)*

Although verse 11 speaks only of "six hundred men" who left, the total number was much larger. Verse 21 speaks of "little ones and the cattle and the carriage" in addition. That is, the six hundred men were accompanied by their families, herds and possessions.

This company moved out from their homes. First they went as far as Kirjath-jearim, east and a little north, not more than ten miles. Apparently they stayed here for some time because the place came to be called "Mahaneh-dan" (camp of Dan) as a result. Probably they made plans and charted their course and strategy there. Then they moved on, coming to the vicinity of Micah's sanctuary. Now the five-man committee made another suggestion. Here was a complete, private sanctuary with a Levite for a priest; so the people must consider what they should do. They could use this ready-made sanctuary in their new city, and they could just as well appropriate it for themselves. The suggestion was accepted.

2. *The Robbery Proper (18:16-21)*

The entire group moved to the sanctuary; then, while the 600 stood at the gate before the building, the five-member committee went inside and began to take the religious articles, including the two main images, the ephod and the teraphim. The Levite stood at the gate with the six hundred, and he only protested when he saw the articles actually being carried from the building. Then they made a proposition to him. Was it better for him to be a priest to one man only or to a tribe and family in Israel (v. 19)? In other words, he was invited to be the priest of the new settlement. This appealed to the man, being the opportunist that he was. Not only did he consent to the robbery but was glad to go with them himself. The whole company moved on, placing the women, children, livestock and possessions at the front, evidently fearing that Micah would pursue them.

Again God's people committed serious sin. Although Micah had no right to make the private sanctuary, neither did these moving Danites have a right to take it away. This was robbery. Perhaps robbery had become common among the people. Micah had robbed his mother and had not been reprimanded for it. Now these Danites robbed Micah. Matters surely were in a serious way in Israel.

3. *The Cry of Micah (18:22-26)*

It is not indicated where Micah was during the robbery. It is implied that he was not present. Possibly the sanctuary was separate from Micah's house; but even so, the commotion made by 600 men would have attracted his attention. Whatever the case, he learned what had happened soon after, and he aroused neighbors to help him pursue the Danites. The group soon caught up with the robbers; but when Micah protested, they asked, "What aileth thee, that thou comest with such a company?" Their attitude was almost one of surprise that he should have objected. This must have been put on, however, for they had taken precautions against this pursuit. When Micah stated what was wrong, they told him not to speak so lest "angry fellows run upon thee, and thou lose thy life, with the lives of thy household." In other words, Micah had better let the matter rest or he would suffer still worse. Micah could only desist, for his group was not large or strong enough to fight the Danites.

This is how the power of numbers affects sin. Greater nations defeat smaller ones in war. The thug with the gun robs the innocent citizen. This sort of thing was transpiring in Israel at this time, compounding the prevalent sin.

E. Establishment of Dan (18:27-31)

The Danite group went on to Laish. Again the force of numbers prevailed as Dan's fighting men defeated those of Laish. Much resistance must have been put up, however, because the Danites burned the city, something they wouldn't have done otherwise since they planned to use it. The city was taken, however; and the Danites moved in, rebuilding it according to their own desires. They changed the name to Dan, after their own tribe and progenitor. There they set up their sanctuary, using the religious articles stolen from Micah. The young Levite served as priest, and here his name is given: Jonathan, the son of Gershom, the son of Manasseh (many manuscripts read "Moses" for "Manasseh"). This false religious arrangement continued "all the time that the house of God was in Shiloh," that is, until the Ark was captured by the Philistines (cf. 1 Sam. 4:4-11). It was wrong to have a sanctuary any place other than at Shiloh.

When one recognizes Israel's sin during this period, he realizes why God found it necessary to withhold His blessing and to permit the times of oppression to come. Sin withheld God's blessing then, and it does the same today. God's people need to realize the awfulness of sin and make every effort to put it away.

Prepare To Answer Intelligently

1. What sin had Micah just committed, as the story of this lesson opens?
2. What did Micah's mother have made with two hundred shekels of silver?
3. What was wrong with the Levite having lived at Bethlehem?
4. Was Micah right in wanting to have a private priest? Explain.
5. What request did the five-man committee make of Micah's private priest?
6. What was attractive about Laish to the committee?
7. How many Danites set out to go and seize Laish?
8. What did they steal from Micah on the way?
9. Why did they do this?
10. What did they quickly establish at Laish?

CHAPTER 13

Civil War in Israel

BIBLE PORTION TO READ: Judges 19:1—21:25

THE SECOND of the two illustrative stories comprises this lesson. Again we see the extent of the sin pervading Israel at this time.

I. The Sin at Gibeah (Judg. 19:1-30)

The account concerns a grievous sin committed by men of Gibeah, in Benjamin, against a Levite and his concubine. Because of this the other tribes of Israel declared war on Benjamin, resulting in great loss of life. This event transpired early in the Period of the Judges. We know this because Phinehas, son of Eleazar, who was active during and even before the time of the conquest (Num. 25:7, 11; Josh. 22:13, 31f), was still the high priest (Judg. 20:28).

A. The Run-Away Concubine (19:1-15)

A certain unnamed Levite lived in Ephraim and took to himself a concubine from Bethlehem. In that day a concubine was a legally wedded wife who held a position secondary to the regular wife. This concubine proved unfaithful to her husband; and, as a result, went to live at her former home in Bethlehem.

After four months, the concubine's husband went after her to bring her back to his house. The concubine seems to have greeted him well, as did her father; for he stayed at the home for three days. On the fourth day he arose to leave with his wife, but the father prevailed on him first to eat again and then to stay one more night. On the fifth day, he again made as though to leave; but the father prevailed on him to stay until afternoon. Then the man left.

Leaving this late in the day, however, the Levite couldn't reach home before nightfall; therefore, he must find a place to lodge. First his servant urged him to find a place in Jerusalem (v. 11), but the Levite refused since it was a place of strangers. (Jerusalem was still held by the Jebusites.) Therefore, they moved on to come to Gibeah just north of Jerusalem. As they entered Gibeah, the sun was setting. No one invited them to stay overnight; so they settled down in "a street" of the city.

Note two things: First, unfaithfulness to a spouse was prevalent in that day; second, hospitality was generous in some homes as witnessed by the Levite's experience in his father-in-law's home.

B. The Kindness of a Man in Gibeah (19:16-21)

During the evening an old man who had been working in the fields came into the city and saw the group sitting together. He wasn't a citizen of Gibeah but was temporarily residing there. In response to the man's query, the Levite told him he had no place to lodge. His reference to "the house of the LORD" probably didn't mean he was going there, for he had just stated that he was going to "mount Ephraim." Rather, since he was a Levite, he had the privilege of going and being received at the Tabernacle; but here in Gibeah he was not being received into any home. The old man invited them to his home, and they went.

Hospitality is a grace that pleases God and should be cultivated by Christians (cf. Rom. 12:13).

C. The Sin of the Gibeahites (19:22-28)

1. *The Story*

Now comes the sin which is the pivotal feature of

the account. This brought about the resultant civil war and terrible loss of life. During the evening hours wicked men of the city came to the house and insisted that the old man deliver to them his guest so they could "know him." This was the same demand that the Sodomites had made of Lot concerning the angels visiting him (Gen. 19:4, 5). The old man, like Lot, defended the honor of his guest; but he offered the men his own virgin daughter and the Levite's concubine. At first the men wouldn't accept the offer. But then they were persuaded and the Levite brought his concubine out to them to do with as they wished.

The evil fellows took her and abused her all night. At dawn they let her go. She got to the door of the house but died there. Her husband found her in the morning when he opened the door to depart. He loaded her body on her donkey and took it to his home.

2. *The Significance*

This story is shocking. The occasion was similar to one occurring centuries earlier at Sodom, only worse. The people of Sodom didn't worship the true God; these did. Also, although the Sodomites were offered Lot's two daughters, they didn't actually get them or abuse them because blindness was imposed on them. Here the Gibeahites abused the young woman shamefully.

The story shows the degree to which sexual sin had become rampant among God's people, indicating that it had been existent and growing for some time. All involved must be condemned. Apparently the old man and the Levite didn't find it difficult to offer these women to the men in exchange for the Levite himself. This had been Lot's case in Sodom. The violation of the woman simply wasn't considered as offensive as the violation of the man. In God's sight either wrong constituted severe sin.

Today God's people live in a world where sexual sins are becoming increasingly prevalent, even among Christians. Many pastors are burdened about sins of this kind in their congregations. God hasn't changed His scale for judging the seriousness of this or any sin. Every child of God should take warning and not let his own mind become calloused toward it.

D. The Other Tribes Are Informed (19:29, 30)

When the Levite reached home, he did a remarkable thing. He cut the body of his dead concubine into twelve parts and sent these to all the tribes. The action yielded results. The other tribes were horrified, saying that nothing like this had happened among the people before; therefore, all should "consider," "take advice" and "speak" their minds.

Sometimes drastic means are necessary to effect drastic actions. The Levite might be charged with showing little love for his concubine by doing this to her body, but at least his action showed his concern with the extent of sin in the land. No doubt he also had in mind other wrongs of similar kind. By sending these pieces of human flesh to the other tribes, he was saying that similar crimes could happen to them unless action were taken; also that this manner of sin existed and would become worse unless something was done. One must at least commend him for his intention. God approves taking action to opposition.

II. Resulting Civil War (Judg. 20:1-48)

A. Assembly of Warriors (20:1-11)

Action did result. Four hundred thousand men assembled at Mizpeh (located in the Benjamite area) in response. These included the leaders. The Levite was also present, and in some detail he told the story of what had happened at Gibeah. He closed with the admonition, "Give here your advice and counsel." The people were ready to act, and they said they would not return home without taking action, proceeding "by lot" (apparently meaning a lot for selecting those of the total 400,000 who would actually fight). They also decided that one-tenth of the population should be asked to supply food for the army (v. 10).

This was a commendable response. The other tribes

could have been indifferent and let the matter go. However, the tribes came together and resolved to do something about the sinful actions. Today's Christians should be as concerned about sin.

B. The Reprehensible Attitude of Benjamin (20:12-16)

First messengers were sent throughout Benjamin to ask that those responsible for the crime be delivered to be punished by death. The Benjamites should have given up the culprits readily. Or if they did not wish to give them up to others, they should at least have meted out punishment themselves. They did neither, however. Rather, they prepared to fight back against the other tribes, apparently believing that their tribe was being unfairly treated. Immediately they began to recruit men for this purpose and assembled as many as 26,000, besides 700 which Gibeah alone provided. Among this total number were 700 who were sufficiently skilled with the sling that they could "sling stones at an hair breadth and not miss" (v. 16).

Being loyal to fellow citizens is one thing; protecting criminals is another. If certain Benjamites had been charged unjustly by the other tribes, one could admire Benjamin for protecting them. However, those charged were guilty of a heinous crime. Thus the Benjamites were protecting perverts and criminals of the worst kind. This was inexcusable.

C. Inquiry of God (20:17, 18)

When Benjamin answered this way, the other tribes rightly sought God's counsel. They went to what is called the "house of God" to do so. The Hebrew phrase is *beth el,* the same as the name of the city Bethel, and probably means that here. Bethel was only about seven miles from Gibeah, whereas Shiloh, where the Tabernacle was located, was about eighteen. The "ark of the covenant" apparently had been brought to Bethel on this occasion to make this inquiry possible (20:27f.). The inquiry would have been made through the high priest (Phinehas, v. 28), using the Urim and the Thummim (Exod. 28:30). The question presented concerned which tribe should go first in attacking Benjamin, and the answer was, "Judah shall go up first."

In any day the child of God should go quickly to God with his needs and problems. Today there is no Urim and Thummim by which to obtain a direct answer, but there is the all-sufficient Word of God; through this, God can and does answer.

D. Israel Twice Defeated (20:19-28)

The battle was joined at Gibeah, the scene of the crime. Apparently the Benjamites led the attack, and they won a decisive victory, killing no less than 22,000 Israelites. The phrase to destroy "down to the ground" means to strike down to the ground in death. Undaunted, the tribes prepared to attack a second time, but first they went to inquire of God once more. They wept as they asked if they should indeed repeat in attacking Benjamin, their brother tribe. Again the response was, "Go up against him." They did so the following day with the same result: There were 18,000 killed this time.

Now "all the people" (apparently only a part had done so earlier) went up to Bethel to seek God's will and favor. They "wept," "sat," "fasted" all day and "offered" sacrifices to God. This showed a greater attitude of humility before God than had been shown the other two times. In fact, here appears to lie the principle difference between this time of inquiry and the first two. At those times, the people seemed to feel they could achieve victory themselves. Now, however, all the people came, wept and fasted. This showed genuine contrition and a sense of dependence. Read God's response in 20:28.

True humility before God is all-important if one is to experience God's blessing. The prayer of the self-confident person is not heard. No matter how able a man may be as the world measures ability, he still is totally dependent on God. God will prosper his use of his ability only as he looks to God in trust. The people had been told to go into battle the first two times, but no victory was promised. Apparently the people still needed to learn humility. Now that this had been learned, they could be promised success.

E. Israel Victorious (20:29-48)
1. *The Story*

Because the third battle proved to be most important, it is described more fully. The description is given in two renditions: a briefer one (vv. 29-36) and a more detailed one (vv. 37-46). The full story must be taken from both renditions.

The tribes moved their army into position on "the third day," probably the third one after the second battle. Before doing so, they placed "liers in wait" (an ambush) near Gibeah, numbering 10,000 (v. 34). The battle joined, and the main forces of the tribes pretended to be defeated before the Benjamites and retreated, bringing the Benjamites away from the city in pursuit. When the ambush saw that the Benjamite army was fully drawn away, these men arose from their hiding place and moved on the city, smiting it with the edge of the sword (vv. 33, 37).

There was a prearranged signal between the two armies of Israel. When the fleeing group should see smoke arising from the city, they should turn and fight those who pursued. The army of ambush then set fire to the city (v. 38), and the fleeing army turned on the Benjamites. At the same time, the Benjamites saw their city burning and recognized that a trap had been sprung against them (v. 40). They turned to flee, going toward the "wilderness" away from both groups of Israelites, headed eastward (v. 43) toward Jericho. They did not get far before "the battle overtook them," and the two groups of Israelites, now joined, slaughtered 18,000.

The surviving Benjamites started toward "the rock of Rimmon" (evidently a high mountain point, affording protection), but along the way about 5,000 more were killed. On reaching a place called Gidom, still short of the "rock of Rimmon," another battle was fought and 2,000 were slain. This made a total of 25,000 (vv. 35, 46). Only 600 remained, and these reached the "rock" where they remained four months.

Israel's troops still didn't cease their slaughter but moved through the land of Benjamin, killing women and children, besides the men who couldn't fight and the livestock. They set fire to the cities, bringing unbelievable destruction and loss of life.

2. *Evaluation*

The strategy the tribes employed in this third battle was much like Joshua's at Ai (Josh. 8). God gave victory, but it is doubtful that He desired anything like the resulting degree of destruction. The Israelites seem to have been carried away by their success. Their thinking seems to have been that since the Benjamites had killed thousands, they should suffer in kind. This should not have been. One must keep a clear head at all times, even in the heat of battle. Much harm can be done by pursuing an end too far.

Great victory did come when the people truly humbled themselves before God. As long as self-confidence characterized them, they were defeated. When they fully trusted God, victory came.

III. Saving the Tribe of Benjamin (Judg. 21:1-25)

A. Remorse for Benjamin (21:1-7)

The other tribes soon regretted what they had done to the tribe of Benjamin. They realized that it might easily become nonexistent. All the Benjamite women had been killed; only six hundred men yet remained; and the tribes had carelessly vowed not to give their daughters to any Benjamite for wives. Thus there was no possibility of children being born.

Once more the people gathered at the house of God, wept and lamented. Now their concern was the harm they had done in carrying the victory too far, a concern they had experienced in other times of gathering. How strange are the ways of God's people. How compassionate is God in His patience with them.

B. Wives from Jabesh-gilead (21:8-15)

Their first solution was to take wives for the Benjamites from Jabesh-gilead. They concluded this after inquiring which tribe had not sent representatives to Mizpeh for the initial meeting regarding Gibeah. Anyone who hadn't been there would not have been party to the oath not to give daughters to the Benjamites; also they would be subject to the death penalty because a "great oath" had been taken at Mizpeh that any not present should be killed. The inquiry revealed that Jabesh-gilead, east of the Jordan, had not been present. Therefore, the men of Jabesh-gilead deserved death; and, being put to death, they wouldn't be able to protect their daughters from being taken as wives for the 600 Benjamites. Accordingly, 12,000 fighters of Israel were selected to go to Jabesh-gilead to mete out the punishment and bring back the virgin daughters. They did this, and 400 virgins were found and brought back. The 600 Benjamites then were summoned from their place of refuge to come peaceably and select wives. They did this, but 200 still remained without wives.

C. Wives from the Daughters of Shiloh (21:16-24)

A plan was now suggested to procure wives for the other two hundred. It was to seize young ladies who annually danced at a "feast of the LORD" in Shiloh. They were called "daughters of Shiloh" and may have been young women who, like the daughter of Jephthah, had been devoted to God for service at the Tabernacle (cf. 1 Sam. 2:22; Luke 2:36, 37). The Benjamites were again summoned and told to go and lie in wait at the place of dancing. When the dancers appeared, each should run quickly and seize the one he wanted. It was also explained that if the girls' fathers or brothers came to complain, the Israelite leaders would defend the Benjamites. The Benjamites carried through the plan, and the remaining two hundred obtained